The Picture Garden Book

Gardens In Color

THE PICTURE GARDEN BOOK
AND GARDENER'S ASSISTANT

GARDENS
IN COLOR

BY

RICHARD PRATT

WITH COLOR PHOTOGRAPHS BY

EDWARD STEICHEN

GARDEN CITY PUBLISHING CO., INC
GARDEN CITY, NEW YORK

1944
GARDEN CITY PUBLISHING CO., INC.

HOWELL, SOSKIN, PUBLISHERS, INC.

17 East 45th Street, New York City

CONTENTS *AND* ILLUSTRATIONS

ILLUSTRATIONS

For Behri

Introduction

All except a very few of the photographs that appear in this book were made by a man whom a multitude of others and I look upon as the finest of all photographs. But in this collaboration I learned to look upon Edward Steichen as being in addition the greatest gardener I know. His help in the preparation of each garden arrangement that we worked upon together was of course inestimable, and I acknowledge it here. For whatever flaws you find in any picture, consider me the culprit.

Gratitude is here again expressed to Mr. David Burpee, who practically turned over Fordhook Farms to us to make some of the early gardens; to Mrs. Ray Levison, who let us use her charming blue and white garden at the late New York World's Fair, and to Helen Van Pelt Wilson, who provided the chapter called Succession of Bloom in a Window Garden.

Most of the gardens illustrated here were planned and executed at what I believe to be the only institution of its kind: a garden project built, equipped and supported by the Ladies' Home Journal on a fortunate farm in Pennsylvania. And for the Journal's decision to endow and operate this widespread studio, with planting fields, greenhouses, workshop and gardener, and for the opportunity thus afforded me to do part of my editorial work at home, I have to thank Bruce Gould and Beatrice Blackmar Gould, as editors of the magazine in which the words and pictures originally appeared; likewise for the permission of the Curtis Publishing Company to use the color plates.

R. P.

New York, March 5, 1942.

Every morning now the ground is covered with a delicate crust that crunches underfoot, and this crust in turn is coated with a sugary blaze, that by noon is all molasses. The one week in the year has arrived when it is better not to meddle with Nature. As far as our garden is concerned, the earth is shedding its skin, or coming out of its cocoon or is just waking up, and doesn't want to be bothered. And I'm in a mood for letting it emerge from its ooze in private. But the gardener, who never gets spring fever, frowns down upon the flower beds that lie there in the fresh warm sunlight as insidious as flypaper, and calls me into conference. As a result of our discussion I have undertaken this year, in addition to my regular routine of spading, raking, weeding and fetching, the following major operations: (a) the compost heap; (b) the poor border; and (c) the wall.

No garden, as the gardener remarked, at least no garden that calls itself a garden, can get along without a compost heap. Nor can it have a flower border with only six inches of soil on top of a solid foundation of hardpan. While a low stone wall that keeps falling down is like a slip that shows.

This is going to be the kind of compost heap that anybody can prepare. Not precisely the alternating layers of upturned sods and manure that a florist or nurseryman might make, but rather a plain backyard heap of anything suitable that comes along from the garden,

lawn or kitchen. It's going to be behind the lilacs, unobtrusive, on a flat spot where the water won't run off, and I'm going to start by digging out a pocket four feet wide by eight feet long, down as far as the good soil goes, which is about eight inches. The excavated sod and soil I'll pile to one side to use on the lower layers. But the first layer that goes in the pocket will be all the dead leaves left from last fall, which will more than fill the hole until I wet them well and tamp them down with my feet. On this layer of leaves I'll sprinkle the seasoning for my compost heap—a dozen handfulls of the following mixture; two parts superphosphate, three parts sulphate of ammonia and four parts ground limestone. This mixture, when soaked down into the layer beneath, not only will help to make humus out of the compost materials, but will give to the eventual humus material a certain fertilizing value and prevent undue acidity.

The process will be repeated, layer by layer, the thickness of each layer depending upon how much I have to put on the heap at any one time, though no single layer will ever be more than five or six inches thick after it is wetted down and tamped. Each layer will be spread evenly over the whole heap and will be slightly concave across the heap so that sprinkling and rainwater will not be wasted. Four feet high will be high enough for the heap, and the material for it, in addition to the first layer of leaves and two layers of the excavated soil with a layer of the sods in between, will be such things as grass cuttings from the lawn, all weeds from the garden which have not gone to seed, vegetable refuse from the kitchen, soil, sods, and whatever else of the kind that comes to hand; only nothing quite so coarse as cornstalks—they don't decompose quickly enough. And on top of each layer that has been pressed and wetted down, a generous, even scattering of the limestone, sulphate of ammonia superphosphate mixture, likewise sprinkled in gently with the hose or watering can.

I'll keep the heap constantly moist—not drenched, and will try to complete it quickly, so it will have the benefit of the summer warmth that accelerates its digestive process, so to speak. If I get it up to full height by the Fourth of July, it will be ready Labor Day to slice down and build into a new pile right alongside—a good morning's job, using the layer method again, scattering on only half as much of the mixture for each layer, and only wetting in the mixture—no tamping down this time. I don't expect the decomposition to be complete by then, but by next spring it will be a fine rich heap of humus. And on Labor Day, too, I will start a new pile in the same spot where the first one was; making the two heaps a continuous operation, year in, year out, and a wonderful source of material with which to tone up all the beds on the place, improving the soil texture and the growing power of the garden immeasurably.

By this time the gardener will have come over from where she was setting out her seedlings and will have taken charge of the work, and I shall have brought over the little bench that she generally sits on for this purpose.

If you have gardened, you will understand how much the prospect of owning that fine supply of compost fills me with indescribable pleasure and excitement.

If it were only ready now, the compost would come in extremely handy for the border that needs to be trenched. This bed is one of four which line a path—two on each side—and form a long, simple garden that flanks the lawn. Each bed is five feet wide and twenty feet long. Three of them have a very decent depth of topsoil, but under the fourth, unluckily, there lies a cropping of shale six inches below the surface, the effect of which upon the plants in that border, is to say the least, quite noticeable. What I want to do in this case is to deepen the topsoil to a full foot, and loosen the subsoil.

Perhaps what I plan to do to this bed, to be accurate and technical, should not be called trenching. That is to say, the two regular ways of trenching do not require getting rid of the subsoil and bringing in topsoil to take its place, which is what I have to do. Conventional method number one is really a renovating job for beds in which the good loam is two spade blades deep—say a foot or so—and where, for the sake of the soil, you put the top six or more inches of soil underneath and the bottom six or more inches on top, loosening up the subsoil as deep as you can.

Conventional method number two is for beds in which the loam is a foot or so deep but in which the bottom six inches or so is neither good enough to put on top nor bad enough to remove altogether. In this case trenching is a matter of taking off the good upper loam, removing two spade widths for a start, then lifting out one width of the lower poor quality loam, loosening up the subsoil with a pick or mattock, spreading compost or manure on the bottom, replacing the lower loam and putting back on top one width of the upper topsoil—proceeding thus right down the bed.

Neither method is for my border, because my undersoil is nothing but solid shale, for which the best thing is removal. So I have got to bring in a load of topsoil from outside—or else rob a five-by-twenty-foot area somewhere on the place—pile it alongside the border and get to work. I shall take about four feet of the border at a time, lift out the plants in that section, strip off the topsoil and pile it in the path, dig out the shale six inches and wheel it away, loosen up the bottom for deep root action and drainage, then throw in the topsoil, mixing the old and the new and adding a little manure. After that I'll replace the plants and proceed. It may sound rather complicated, but you must remember that it will all be simplified for me by the gardener, who will be there on her bench passing out directions.

Now that I've thought it over, I'm not so sure I'll get around to the wall this summer. By the time I've begun the compost heap and trenched the border the heat will be here, and a wall is nothing for warm weather. Besides, there will be weeding, watering, cultivating and lawn mowing, not to mention a lot of odd jobs to do for the gardener. As a matter of fact, I think I hear her calling me now.

Seeds to sow on a false-spring day

Most annual seeds have a line on the packet advising you to plant them outside only after all danger of frost is over. But I'm talking now about the tough ones that the gardener sticks in the ground as soon, sometimes, as March, when she begins keeping her eye on the soil the way a robin watches for a worm; the reason for this vigil being that there aren't many moments this early in the year when the earth, in a horticultural sense, is fit to touch. She'll run out about noon of a good day and pick up a handful of loam from the place where she wants to plant. If it squeezes into a soft cake, like a piece of putty, she throws it down in disgust. But if it crumbles in her hand, she gives a cry of delight that could be a primitive song of spring, and calls for me to bring her whole basket of tools, which has been standing ready in the hallway for weeks, and the scrap of carpet or the board on which she kneels when the ground is cold. In her excitement, neither one of us can find the seeds, till she discovers them in her hand, where they've been all morning.

The big event is getting in the sweet peas, but I'll come back to this later. First, here are the annuals whose seeds the gardener likes to get in the ground early—the earlier the better, within reason; the reason to consider being what damage, or rather disarrangement, might be caused the shallow-planted seeds by the torrents of spring. Mere frost is no danger to the seeds of corn-flower, calendula, kochia (that feathery-foliage plant called summer cypress), sweet alyssum, larkspur, calliopsis and poppies. In fact, these annuals could be planted in the fall, as far as that goes; only the gardener has never had very good luck with her fall planting—the seeds seeming to wash away, or wash into tight little clusters. This she prevents almost entirely in early spring planting by covering them with a piece of burlap, which breaks the force of heavy rains.

She sows the seeds in winter-cold ground that I've worked up to a depth of at least six inches yet whose surface is dry enough to pulverize. It takes care-ful watching, as I've said, to catch it in this condition so early in the season, and it doesn't usually stay this way long. The gardener sows in rows or in scat-tered array, depending upon the effect she wants to get; covers the seeds with a good quarter inch of fine soil, then firms the surface with the palm of her hand.

She plants her sweet peas much more deeply, scattering them zigzag along a furrow three inches deep and six inches wide; first having called me in to spade the whole row as far down as the good soil goes, loosening up the bottom, too, if it is hard. Well-rotted manure, or plenty of bone meal, is worked into the soil below, and after the seeds are cov-ered a dressing of lime is raked into the top surface.

The bamboo stakes for the lattice are six feet long. You make two rows, a foot or so apart, of crisscrossed stakes, stuck firmly in the ground and fastened together near the top. At various times we've used other means of support: chicken wire, string, a wide-mesh net-ting made especially for the purpose, and brush. They're all adequate; the bamboo being the neatest, we think—but a very scarce wartime article. The thing is not so much the type of support; it's the way the sweet peas perform. And that goes for garden peas as wel'

The problem of paths

As far as I am concerned, March is a month to be spent in making up your mind what to do from April on. And while the gardener is occupied with her two-leaf sprouts of petunias, transfer-ring them from seed pans to thumb pots, I am contemplating, among other things, the problem of paths.

For while the gardener's body is at the bench, I know her mind is in all the far corners of the garden and lawn—where the clusters of early spring-flowering bulbs we planted last September are now tantalizingly in bloom. Yet if she were to try to reach them in this season of thaw, with the turf in its current car-amel-like condition, it would take me the rest of the summer to get rid of her footprints.

What I shall recommend is a stepping-stone footpath that skirts the front of the shrubbery where it meets the lawn. For paths like this that are mostly a wet-weather way through the grass, I like a dotted line better than a solid one; for a string of flagstones, set an easy footstep apart, doesn't disturb the status of the lawn. In the garden itself, however, where the straight path be-tween flower beds is a part of the plan, I'd rather see the solid idea carried out with full, even width, neat edge and squared corners.

There is quite a range of materials for garden paths of the regular variety, including gravel, tile, brick, stone; but I think I shall try tanbark chips, which make a firm but springy surface that dries off quickly, and give off a delightfully pungent fragrance when damp from rain or dew. But whatever I use for the surface, the foundation, which is the part that keeps the path solid and dry, will be eight or more inches of broken stone and cinders.

In a path with a surface of loose material, like tanbark or gravel, it is a good plan to have an edging on either side to keep the borders neat. This can be made with boards, brick, tile or stone. I shall line my tanbark path on either side with four-inch cypress boards, set into the ground on edge, showing about an inch; so that when the gardener is cultivating, she won't get the flower beds into the tanbark, and vice versa.

And as I ponder the problem of my steppingstone path, one of the possibilities I am considering is that of using foot-square blocks of pecky cypress instead of actual flat stones. These cypress blocks are sawed about three inches thick against the grain, and are made especially for paths, being almost as everlasting as stone. They soon tone to a fine, earthy, grass-stained color, and make an ideal retiring footway for the lawn, where a more conspicuous path would interrupt the green "flow" of which the gardener is so rightly fond.

Under each one of the blocks or stones I shall prepare a foundation similar in depth and materials to the one prescribed for the garden path. For it is just as important here that the path

should be solid, and a good foundation is the only guaranty of this. And as I have said, the distance from the center of one stone or block to the next center should be no greater than a person can cover in an easy step. Already, because of these new paths in my mind, the gardening work ahead of me for the season has begun to seem very simple and pleasant, everything much closer than before —including the crocuses.

Getting down to earth

The gardener picks up a handful of dirt from the flower bed and squeezes it. She has been doing this for days, like a cook with a broom straw, but each time until now the loam has formed a more or less solid lump in her palm. On this occasion, however, it crumbles, and as it falls away between her fingers she gives me a certain glance. Her look is something more than a signal for me to get ready for gardening; it is in a way the first absolute sign of spring.

The robin, the crocus, the new warm sunlight and the inevitable languor can all be false alarms so far as getting out the fork and trowel is concerned. For while the gardener has been busy for weeks straightening up after winter, it would never occur to her to do any actual digging, or let any be done, until the ground was what the garden books call "friable." This is when the soil pulverizes nicely in the hand; neither clammy, as it is apt to be in early spring, nor baked or powdery as during a dry spell.

At any rate, the soil in the garden has now at last achieved that desirable texture. And with a basket and wheelbarrow filled with tools wiped clean of winter oil we make our way to the twenty-foot section of border which is waiting for the spade.

I am afraid it has been waiting for several years, it never having been properly prepared in the first place. It is an odd little area, filled in, partly, over an old foundation, neglected so far as any conscientious cultivation is concerned, and used by the gardener as a cutting patch for annuals. In fact, it contains practically every fault you're likely to encounter in connection with soil.

One part of it is almost pure clay, another is gravelly, and the rest is a very thin layer of fairly good soil on a shale bottom. The gravelly part drains off too well, the clay part not well enough. But I must say that in spite of this poor border's various drawbacks the gardener's annuals have always done rather nicely in it—proving to us that these plants in general are not the least bit finical. And I am not going to do anything very fancy to it now; just give it a good enough start so that it can keep on improving itself.

First I am going to go over it with a mattock, which is a double-edged digging tool, like a pickax, except that the blades are flat and fairly sharp. I shall loosen the whole bed to a depth of about fifteen inches—the deeper the better, for the farther down you thoroughly disturb the soil, the more available you make its nourishment, facilitate drainage, and thus encourage good root growth. As a rule, deeply worked soil gets better all the time, making the extra effort well worth while.

The mattock will break up the clay, will even break up the shale hardpan that lies under the shallow soil. Large pieces of shale and all sizable stones I shall take away in the wheelbarrow, and shall bring back in their place good soil, compost and manure.

When the mattock work is finished I shall rest for a while, then with the spading fork I shall turn the whole bed over again to mix in the spreading of new soil and manure and break up any lumps I may have missed with the mattock. Every four or five feet down the bed I shall drop the fork and use the rake on the part I have just finished spading, as raking goes much better when it is done on freshly spaded ground; also it's a relief to change off.

There is no such thing as too much raking, so when the bed has been finished as described above I shall first give it a generous coating of my favorite fertilizer—bone meal, which is slow-acting but safe—then rake it again.

Then I shall turn the bed over to the gardener, who will be ready by this time to set out her seedlings from her thumb pots. On this well-prepared ground she will have no difficulty getting them to prosper, and without any further preparation she can also plant her seeds of sweet alyssum, portulaca and Shirley poppies, which like to be planted right where they are going to grow.

The gardener's springboard

The gardener has a light piece of plywood, about the size of a chair seat, padded on one side, too, and covered with oilcloth. On this she kneels when she gets down to work in the garden,

and also she uses it for sitting on, say when the top of the stone wall is damp and cold, and I am doing something nearby that she wants to follow. She calls it her springboard, because spring is about the only time of the year she bothers with it. As soon as the ground warms up she gets right down on the dirt.

Springboard is a good name for it another way as well, for from it on these first delightful days she plunges right into her gardening. Every time I go that way, there she is, arching over into the ripples of fresh ground. Behind her stands the wheelbarrow, loaded down with paraphernalia, a lot of which she'll never touch. For while she trundles quite a few tools off to work every morning, the only two pieces of equipment with which she's really occupied right now are the springboard and the slender claw. With this latter implement she can, if she kneels down, do just the kind of careful cleaning up that at this time any flower bed requires.

And because of the springboard, which makes it possible with warm, dry knees, to get close to the ground, where no tender shoots escape the eye, and because of the lithe cultivator, which can be drawn with great delicacy among the shoots, the whole operation of spring gardening is brought clearly into focus.

This gardener first of all removes the remains of the winter mulch—that is, everything that doesn't scratch readily into the surface of the soil. The same with all dead leaves and stalks that haven't already rotted away into good humus for the ground. She trims away what's left of last year's iris leaves; draws out the dry debris of dead petunias; claws up the clinging chickweed,

and together with all weeds whatsoever she uproots the tiny seedlings of the tall garden phlox, which will only turn out to be a mean magenta anyway. Then onto this scratched-over ground she sprinkles a good garden fertilizer, and works it into the new receptive surface.

Gradually she gets the garden good and neat, and gives it its first spread of nourishment. If there are empty spaces for which she has no other special plans, she scatters in a few packets of annual seeds, of things which like to grow where they're planted—larkspur, Shirley poppies, nicotiana. In among the new narcissus foliage is another place for annual seeds that will be coming up, as, later on, these leaves come fading down. Or if she has brought any boxes of ageratum or verbena up indoors, or any other annual plants at all, she will set out some of the seedlings in among these empty places.

Then, as she comes to the larger clumps of chrysanthemums, hardy asters, delphiniums and the tall garden phlox, she digs them up, one at a time, and tenderly takes them apart. Sometimes a large chrysanthemum clump, covered in spring with new leafy shoots, will produce from a dozen to fifty small plants, each one capable of becoming a full-sized plant by fall. Phlox and delphinium aren't quite so prolific of small plants by division, but each large clump should considerably increase your supply if you disengage the several crowns of whch you will find each main cluster is composed. And by this method of propagation you may be sure that you will preserve in each case the exact colors and characteristics of the mother plants, something which can't be done

[Continued on page 22]

Tulip Garden

Tulips are all shades of red, yellow, lavender, pink, mahogany and purple, with many interminglings, so it takes considerable will power to plant nothing but white ones unless this garden persuades you to do so at planting time this fall. For while there are here quite a few forget-me-nots, azaleas and pansies, the white tulips are what make it. The white-and-blueness is important, too, as any simple color scheme in a garden always is. The easy waving line of forget-me-nots is a graceful idea; the dwarf box edging contributes its fine antique fragrance; the tanbark path provides a strip of springy, pungent carpeting, while the azaleas (indica alba) make a spotless background. And the nice part about it is you can get the same effect somewhere in a corner, on a smaller scale, with a dozen tulips, a basket or two of pansy plants, a packet of dwarf forget-me-not seed, no boxwood necessarily, and a single plant of azalea. The tulips here are the May-flowering Glacier, White Giant, and Mrs. Grullemans.

Tulips are among the showiest of all garden flowers. They grow from bulbs that are planted in the fall, and if left undisturbed, and if undamaged by poor drainage, rodents or disease, they will keep on coming up satisfactorily for about four years—sometimes more, sometimes less.

Tulips begin blooming in April, or before, with the species, or "wild" types, and the Early Tulips, and run through May with the Cottage and Darwin types. It is these latter May-flowering tulips, tall, lasting and beautifully colored, which make the tulip such a famous and favorite garden flower.

In buying the bulbs where you can look them over, select those which are firm and plump and sound at the base. Shriveled bulbs have lost some of their vitality. As a rule, the larger and heavier the bulbs, the better, but perfectly satisfactory results are to be had without paying too high a premium for extreme size.

The bed should be prepared a few weeks before planting time, so that the ground will settle. Spade the soil with well-rotted manure or bone meal pretty late in the fall—about two or three weeks before the first real frost. In this way the bulbs are not encouraged by a spell of Indian summer to start growing in the face of winter.

No animal manures should be used unless they are thoroughly decayed, as they may cause the plant to rot and in some instances favor the development of diseases. All fertilizers should be thoroughly mixed with the soil as they may injure the bulbs or the new growth if placed where they come into direct contact with them.

When bulbs are to remain in the ground all winter, adequate drainage is more essential for them than for bulbs planted in the spring and taken up again in the fall. Low spots are to be avoided.

Arrange the tulips in rows, the bulbs eight inches apart, with each kind and variety together. Tulips look the most effective in beds or groupings of the same color, with perhaps a half a dozen different colors in corners here and there. After setting out the bulbs in their proper positions on the surface of the soil, dig the holes exactly six inches deep to the bottom of the bulbs, unless you are planting early tulips, in which case the holes should only be five inches in depth.

A handy tool for digging the holes is a bulb planter, which resembles a large apple corer. You plunge it in the ground to the proper depth, and when you lift it out the soil comes up with it, leaving a nice clean hole for the bulb. Or you may prefer to use a trowel.

If you like to be careful with your bulbs, dig the holes an inch deeper and put an inch of sand in the bottom. This will prevent rotting if the soil is inclined to be damp. And as mice consider tulip bulbs a great delicacy, it is a good plan to sprinkle the bulbs with napthalene flakes. If you use manure with the planting, be sure and mix it with the soil beneath the bulb and not above it.

If it has been necessary to do the planting late and the soil is dry, it is important to water the soil thoroughly enough for the moisture to soak down to the bulb, in order to produce the quick development of the roots. Once the roots are established, cold, wet soil and hard freezing will not be injurious, but the bulbs which are not thoroughly rooted cannot so well withstand these conditions.

On top of the first frost, spread a light mulch of salt hay, straw, or this new glass wool that looks like cotton batting. The mulch helps to hold in the frost, prevents the surface of the soil from washing, "puddling," or heaving during the winter or early spring, and also serves to check the bulbs from starting too quickly in the event of prematurely warm weather in February or March.

The mulch should be worked into the ground, or removed, when the tips of the leaves start to come through in the spring. Also, the surface of the soil between the bulbs, packed hard after the winter's storms, should be lightly cultivated or loosened up. For this purpose one of the small fingered or pronged hoes, on a long handle, is most convenient.

When the bulbs have finished blooming, they restore their energy for the next season through the foliage above. For this reason the leaves should never be cut off until they turn yellow and start to drop, which usually takes two to three weeks or more.

If you want to use the bed for other flowers after the tulips have gone, you can dig up the bulbs as soon as they are finished blooming and set them close together in a six-inches-deep furrow. Cover them up, with the leaves exposed, and let them ripen. Then when the leaves are dried, dig up the bulbs, let them dry off, and store them away until fall in a dry cool cellar.

Or you can make use of your tulip bed by planting the seeds of some quick and easy annual like marigolds or zinnias, or set out some small plants like verbena or petunias, which would be grateful for the shade of the tulip leaves until the leaves are ready to be trimmed off at the ground; after which, with very little delay, there will be a very nice bed of flowers.

Blooms from tulip bulbs left in the ground from year to year hardly improve in quality, nor is it possible to achieve perfection by digging them up and replanting them in the fall. The best plan is to plant new bulbs every three or four years, leave them in the ground with interplantings of annuals, and when they begin to wear out put in another supply.

The colors of tulips range from the softest of pastels to buoyant red and salmon, with a shade to suit everyone. Some of the more popular varieties are as follows:

A TULIP GARDEN

GOOD VARIETIES OF DARWIN TULIPS

Prince of Wales, bright rosy crimson, 30"
Pride of Haarlem, brilliant rose carmine, 28"
Kathleen Parlow, true pink with silver margins, 30"
Princess Elizabeth, clear deep pink, 28"
Clara Butt, clear pink, flushed salmon-rose, 22" (one of the best)
Glacier, one of the best whites, rather expensive, 31"
Mrs. Grullemans, large creamy white, also not cheap, 27"
Zwanenburg, pure white, very popular, 23"
The Bishop, soft violet-purple, 29"
La Tulipe Noire, very dark maroon-black, darkest of all, 26"
Reverend Ewbank, soft lavender-violet, 23"

GOOD VARIETIES OF COTTAGE TULIPS

Vesta, a wonderful white for garden and cutting, 28"
Picotee, white with deep rose margins, 24"
Inglescombe Pink, soft rosy pink, 25"
Scarlet Emperor, immense bright scarlet, 23"
Mrs. Moon, rich golden yellow, 25"
Inglescombe Yellow, canary, with scarlet margins when in full bloom, 23"
Illuminator, deep yellow flushed with scarlet, 24"

GOOD VARIETIES OF SINGLE EARLY TULIPS

White Beauty, just about the best white, 12"
White Swan, pure white, eggshaped, less expensive, 15"
Pink Beauty, pink-margined white, turning to rose, 12"
Proserpine, carmine-rose, 14"
De Wet, golden yellow, flushed with orange, a beauty, 16"
Duc Van Thol, scarlet, very dwarf and early, 8"
Van der Neer, brilliant violet-purple, 12"
Keizerskroon, crimson-scarlet with yellow border, 16"
Goldfinch, deep yellow, fragrant, 13"

by seed—at least by the seed of these four particular favorites.

Of course, all this careful application of the gardener's has a wonderful effect. Borders that are woebegone one day are polished up the next. Every veteran plant or new recruit suddenly seems full of pride and self respect. The litter of winter is gone; the waxy, weatherworn surface of the soil no longer smothers the roots underneath. The good loam looks as though it could breathe again. And the gardener comes into the house, drops the springboard and the claw in the closet, and collapses into a chair. While I go out and bring back the wheelbarrow.

Annuals in pots, just in case

There was a time when she would go out and buy her plants, just about to bloom, or even already in flower. The cost was trifling, but now that what used to be a bother has become part of the fun she goes ahead on her own.

These plants in pots come in handy for last-minute places where you suddenly find you need an immediate effect. The seed is sown outside, at the same time as the other annuals, but instead of leaving them to grow where they were planted, the gardener lifts them tenderly from the ground as soon as their second pair of leaves has appeared. She then plants the ones with the best roots in inch pots, one plant to a pot. On a level piece of prepared bed she presses the pots about an inch into the soft soil, one against the next in close array, so they can be easily cared for as a cluster.

This care consists of a little shade for the first few days—a sheet of newspaper laid lightly over them is enough, and occasional watering. But water should be applied at first only in a fine spray, so the fragile seedlings won't be battered down, just enough watering to keep the soil dampish in the pots. And of course as soon as the little plants have begun a sturdy growth, she does away with the nursing, lets them harden off, as they say.

This spring the gardener has improved her method by fixing up a level bed, three by six, of cinders, mixed with a little peat moss to hold the moisture. This is better than soil, because it doesn't get muddy or hard, and doesn't grow weeds. And to shade the potted seedlings I have made a lath screen—ordinary wooden laths, three feet long, double-nailed at each end to a three-by-one-inch strip six feet long, each lath a lath width away from its neighbors. Three stakes, a foot high, along the front and the back of the bed support the screen, which is removed when the potted seedlings get their full strength.

In from four to six weeks the gardener has a collection of well-developed plants which can be placed anywhere she needs them, and even though they are about to bloom, some, in fact, beginning to bloom, there is no danger that setting them out from their pots into the ground can have any bad effect. For by this time each plant has plenty of roots, and as these roots are scarcely disturbed in the transfer from the pot to the garden, they grow on as if nothing had happened. The only trick is to squeeze gently the pot-shaped form of soil that emerges, so that the tight angle of roots will be loosened up a little and have a chance to take hold in the ground.

Now it is perfectly true that these same plants can be grown just as easily in the ground; but as the season advances it becomes more and more difficult to move them with complete success. Most annuals sown where they are to grow need a certain amount of thinning out. The plants acquired in this thinning-out process the gardener now and then sticks in elsewhere. Sometimes, when she hits a streak of overcast weather, this type of transplanting works very well. Even in the heat, with careful watering, pinching back and a little luck, she has experienced fair success. But the plants from pots almost invariably flourish. And anyhow, she likes to raise them this way, which is reason enough.

Almost any of the annuals she raises in this fashion. And the potting method need not be merely an early season expedient. Plants of most annuals, started up to July, potted at the second-leaf stage, and watered and shaded with discretion, have provided the gardener with fresh material for run-down places in the garden right up until fall. And whenever she needs something at the blooming point, in a hurry, there it is, in the little colony of potted plants she keeps on hand for just this purpose.

Gardening with annuals

The gardener, you gather, is a great one for annuals, always getting more seeds than she really needs, but managing in the end to make excellent use of every packet. At first it took some urging on her part to persuade me to make the various places ready for planting, but now I am afraid it is I who lead her on. It is kind of fun to see what she will do with the spots I prepare.

It goes something like this. As soon as the ground is ready for working, which is when it crumbles nicely in the hand, I search out every bare spot on the place—in front of the shrubbery, against the fence, along the walks and the wall, beside the house, even in among the perennials. If there is room to spade, I do a job of preparation; if the space is too small for spading, or too cramped, I do the best I can with a hoe. Then I rake the surface to a fine finish, and as some of our soil is still inclined to crust over, I sprinkle sand over the surface and rake that gently in or work in humus to improve the friability. This makes an easy seedbed to sow. In addition to these odd places, I create an entirely new bed every now and then, in some corner that looks as though it could stand some color. And no matter how small or obscure the spots I have prepared, the gardener has never yet failed to find them all and fill them with seeds.

Rather, it is more as though she waved a wand over these bare spots. For there is something magical about the way certain annuals suddenly grow into leaf and flower from a package of seeds. And now that the gardener has acquired the knack of fitting in the right kinds of flowers where they will be most effective, the whole place is beautifully garnished by June, and becomes more so as summer and fall progress.

As a general rule, she plants all her annual seeds to a depth four times their diameter, or smallest dimension if flat.

And she usually plants them either broadcast or in a pattern of interweaving furrows. She covers the seed carefully with a suitable film of fine soil, then tamps the bed with the bottom of her garden rake.

Her favorites are verbena and phlox drummondi for places where low, semi-trailing plants are suitable, and she likes to plant them in clusters of separate colors—reds and whites of both and the brilliant purple blues of verbena. She has a weakness for the single white portulacas, and every summer the dry, hot strip along the top of a wall is covered with these creeping, wild-rose-like flowers nestling in their succulent foliage. Petunias are another one of her passions, the ordinary singles especially, and of these she prefers the soft pink Rosy Morn, the new blue Glamor Girl, and the pure white Snow Queen. Here again she groups the colors, rather than making an indiscriminate melange; and she keeps her petunias in beds to themselves.

She has three favorite annuals which she always buys in mixtures. These are Shirley poppies, larkspurs and zinnias. She likes the poppies for places large enough to mass their pastel shades effectively, and protected enough to keep their delicate petals from being whipped by the wind. The larkspurs she likes to plant in little bays of the shrubbery, where their tall spikes and feathery foliage cut against the bank of leafage behind them, a pleasant change from the conventional edging. She uses nothing now but the new Giant Imperials. As for zinnias, she covers any awkward slope with them which needs covering, the larger the mass the better; anything, she says, rather than setting them out in regular rows, which is the way I'd plant them. And for robust purpose she plants the mixture of California Giants, with their five-inch flowers in a dozen brilliant colors.

This seems a paltry list of annuals, considering what you encounter in the catalogues; and I don't pretend it covers the gardener's ground. As a matter of fact, she does quite a little with cornflowers, sweet William, marigolds and the large single China asters, but mostly for cutting. And of course she tries out six or eight new things every season. I never know just what is going to come up in the places I prepare, but it is always a pleasant surprise.

The hungry garden

In the beginning the gardener was inclined to pamper the ground with all sorts of delicacies. She was so grateful to the soil for the way it sent up her seeds that she fed it from spring to fall with every new fertilizer she could find. If you can call any fertilizer a delicacy.

Sometimes it would be only a snack from a sample package, for the place around a certain plant, and sometimes it would be the better part of a ten-pound bag to make a spread for the whole border; but either way it would be given more as a treat than as absolute manna. For I made it my business whenever I put the garden through its spring workout with the spade to turn in plenty of manure, with a liberal raking of bone meal on the surface to boot, so there seemed to me really no crying necessity for all this extra fare.

Yet in many cases I must admit the results were rather amazing. Plants to which the gardener gave a stimulating

24

spoonful of fertilizer seemed to spring without delay into leaf and flower; even coming out, she claimed, in finer colors than those which failed to receive this favor.

She found, of course, that it was fatal to linger over the long list of fertilizers in the seed catalogues. There was a limit to this type of temptation, and the gardener soon reduced this limit to a single brand that seems to serve her purpose very well.

So in our garden larder now there is this one brand of quick-acting fertilizer which the gardener uses to give her seedlings a lift and to stimulate her tall perennials just before they are about to bloom. It could be any one of several kinds a reliable dealer would be glad to recommend, and it is practically equivalent to the 4-12-4 formula you buy in bulk at any large garden-supply place—the figures meaning the percentages present of nitrogen, phosphoric acid and potash, respectively.

The rest of the garden larder consists of a hundred-pound bag of dehydrated and pulverized cow manure, a rather ritzy way to buy this material, yet very practical for the small place; a similar-sized bag of bone meal; a bale of pulverized peat moss; a large sack of leaf mold; a bag of finely ground limestone; and a small pile of sand in the corner. And I don't care how bad a piece of ground the gardener wants me to make into good growing beds, with these ingredients it can be done. With the bone meal and manure a poor piece of lawn can soon be whipped into shape. With the peat moss and sand I can lighten the heaviest kind of clay. With the leaf mold, sand, some garden loam and a little bone meal I can make a mixture for pots and flats which no seed or plant could possibly resist.

For the beginner who wants to experiment in a small way with soil improvement by means of these various fertilizers and conditioners, it is possible to get them in moderate quantities at no great cost; and they are certainly one of the best investments a person can make.

The gardener has learned a few simple facts in addition to the one that quick-acting fertilizer should be used with discretion. She has learned that peat moss, while an excellent soil conditioner for soil that is either too light or too heavy, contains no nourishment, and that too much of it in the garden is apt to produce acidity. She has learned to use lime early in the season, never to mix it with fertilizer, which it weakens, nor to use it on lawns if it encourages weeds, and not to use it with broad-leaved evergreens, which like an acid soil that lime tends to sweeten. She has learned that bone meal, while slow-acting, is one of the safest and most reliable fertilizers available; that leaf mold scratched into the surface of the garden soil keeps it from caking and helps to hold the moisture; and that the more manure I spade into the garden every spring the better everything seems to grow, regardless.

Gardening in a barrel

A year ago the gardener produced an empty barrel and got me to bore it full of two-inch holes, and quite a job it was, cutting through those hard oak staves, but that wasn't all. I had to bore small holes in the bottom of the barrel for

[Continued on page 33]

A Garden's Four Seasons

Behind the beauty of this garden, with its stream of color that flows from frost to frost, lies a lesson in the art of gardening for anyone with a problem in planting or planning. It is really a series of lessons, beginning with a plot of ground as plain as a piece of paper, and ending with a flower parade that fills the panels without a pause from early April until late November. The unbroken succession of bloom, which has been caught so convincingly in the four photographs, will seem to many people the most important part in the garden's development, for it is, of course, a fact that continuous color is the goal of every earnest gardener. But the creation of a setting for this display and the arrangement of the various elements and features were just as essential to the final effectiveness. And in this garden all these things have been achieved with such simplicity and directness that every step from outset to finish can, with suitable variations, be followed to guide the evolution of any garden, regardless of size, situation or cost.

The photographs fail in one respect: they give no indication of how the garden has progressed in the last sixteen years from an unadorned site to a finished design, as an empty canvas becomes a colorful painting. The garden began to take shape as a rectangular space, rolled out like an immense rug in front of the house, bordered by a low wall, and enclosed in a dense planting of white birches, flowering cherries, and dogwoods. Where formerly there was no shade, no protection from the wind, and no feeling of seclusion, there is now a generous supply of these important requirements, all furnished by a surrounding grove that at the same time provides the garden with a beautiful frame. Within that frame the garden is treated as a carpet of turf on which is laid a simple pattern of flower beds. At the far end, against a background of birches, a garden seat stands as an open invitation, symbolizing the fact that this garden is not only an amiable

SPRING. *The curtain rises on tall battalions of tulips in rose, red, scarlet, pink and white.*

LATE SUMMER. *A delicate scheme of pastel colors characterizes the garden's third act.*

EARLY SUMMER. *The second act is dominated by the clear colors of peonies and iris.*

FALL. *A riot of chrysanthemums brings the performance to a close with an exciting flourish.*

diversion and pleasant decoration, but a spacious outdoor room in which it is possible to rest and entertain.

This part of the garden arrangement—the surrounding growth of trees, the bordering walls, the seat in a bower of green and white, the pattern of beds and tapis vert—is the setting for the performance that is played by the flowers. The show begins with a prologue of snowdrops and crocuses. Spots and patches of pink and blue and white appear in the borders and along the sunny sides of the walls before the last of the snow has gone. The garden composition is just as clear-cut in winter as it is in summer, due to the architectural quality of its framework of woods and walls, but the first exciting moment of the year is when these starlike flowers begin to poke above the ground in scattered constellations of color. And when the curtain of spring actually rises, and the tulips make their stunning entrance, the spectacle has really commenced.

The climax of the first act occurs in the middle of May. Then the beds are brilliant with Darwin and Breeder tulips; tall-stemmed battalions of rose and red and scarlet. Graceful clusters of bleeding-hearts, white edging of candytuft and achillea, and purple strips of the little Jersey Gem viola make up a colorful supporting cast. Against the fresh green foliage around the garden the dogwood flowers hang in great garlands of pink and white.

The scene changes gradually, but without any diminishing of the color scheme, as the irises and peonies appear. By the middle of June the chromatic effect has altered from a general tone of rose and white to a combination of yellow, white, blue and lavender. In addition to the peonies and irises, there are now delphinium and foxglove, and along the edges of the borders are rows of the pink dianthus named Beatrice. One of the most effective flower groups at this time is the cluster of yellow foxgloves which stands in the semi-shade beyond the garden seat.

By late summer the principal roles are being played by the gladioli, phlox, tall blue masses of veronica, new varieties of day lilies, boltonia, the fine pink Lilium speciosum rubrum, and the various annuals which have taken the place of the tulips . Among the last the most important are many plants of the long-blooming aster frikarti. This is a season when gardens are apt to lose their color,

31

amounting at times almost to an intermission, but here the late-summer performance is as lovely as any other part of the spectacle. It has a pastel beauty which is altogether distinct in quality from that of any other month of the garden year.

And it is especially effective as a prelude to the final act. The soft and quiet aspect of late summer begins to turn at the first suspicion of frosty nights to the thrilling colors of the chrysanthemums. As the background of birches, dogwoods, and cherries takes on its autumn tints these fall flowers are moved, in full bloom, from where they have been growing all summer in the vegetable garden. In the borders they are given the places of the annuals, now practically gone, which were in turn used to carry on the work of the tulips. Their colors range from pure white through yellow, orange, gold and bronze, to all the reds from pink to crimson, and the effect is almost indescribable.

This thrilling finish to the garden year is made possible by the use of a new race of early-flowering chrysanthemums developed within the past decade. It is due also to the ease with which these plants can be moved from outside the garden proper, where by judicious pinching back and careful cultivation they have been made ready for this September transplanting that gives the garden its stupendous finale.

drainage, make a square tube of narrow boards which would take care of the drainage down through the center length of the barrel, bore that full of holes and fill it with excelsior. The next thing was to set the barrel, open end up, on four bricks, like feet; and then, while the gardener held the excelsior-filled core in place down the middle of the barrel, I filled the barrel with an equal mixture of garden soil, leaf mold and sand.

The large holes in the sides of the barrel were staggered about a foot apart all around from top to bottom, and in each one of them the gardener set a plant of an alpine strawberry—Baron Solemacher. And after a few weeks of conscientious watering from the top, I must say the barrel began to look rather beautiful. The strawberry plants got bushier and bushier, and seemed to be in flower and fruit, simultaneously, all summer.

It was an odd idea, but would be a practical one where space was limited, and the effect was quaint and attractive enough so that we shall keep on planting the barrel every spring, though not necessarily with strawberries. This year the gardener put petunias in the holes and planted ageratum on top. Next year it will be either nasturtiums or some of those cherrylike tomatoes.

When the gardener brought the barrel home and explained her plan, I remembered having seen the same kind of thing done with wooden tubs or barrels sawed in half; the holes in the sides filled with sempervirens—those succulent-leaved plants called houseleeks, or hen-and-chickens or old-man-and-woman, according to your locality. These eccentric plants are ideal for the tub

or barrel garden, as their queer forms and habits of growth fit right into the whole fantastic notion. I say "fantastic," though I am very fond of the barrel garden, now that it is made, and all I have to do with it is to turn it around a little every once in a while to give all the plants a chance at the sun.

Someone who saw the gardener's barrel garden sent her from the South a pottery strawberry jar. It is pretty much the same in principle, but, having been made for the purpose, was all ready to use, I am glad to say. The gardener has filled it with some more of my potting mixture, and is now in the midst of planting pansies in its open mouths.

Spur-of-the-moment versus planning ahead

When the gardener gets an idea, she likes to put it into practice right away. All of a sudden she will pull up a poor plant and put a—presumably—better one in its place. Or without any warning she will appear with a spade and show me where to make a bed for some marigolds that have turned out too well for the cutting patch. This I think is all wrong. I feel that a gardening decision should be made with great deliberation, preferably in the shade, sitting down, even if it takes all afternoon.

But in spite of her impulsiveness, the gardener has always been so lucky that I have never been able to convince her completely of the wisdom of premeditated planning. However, the evidence of the perennial border this season may persuade her to switch her point of view. Heretofore this border has been her special province. Of course, it never had any particular color scheme; it was just an assortment of scattered inspirations, overcrowded in spots and suddenly sparse in others—though she was able in every emergency to remedy the situation on the spur of the moment. And I must admit that the effect, while somewhat disordered was generally gay. In appearance it was a picnic—not a table set with course after course.

The garden, as I have planned it now, begins with pink and white tulips, in rows a foot apart, and a foot apart in the rows, set out very carefully with a line, and each tulip marked with a six-inch wooden label, stuck in the ground in back of the bulb. This may sound a little formal and particular; but as a matter of fact, it is very practical. When the tulips are planted and marked, they give you a splendid guide for the rest of your planting. And now that they have finished flowering, and the iris and columbine are coming into bloom, I am taking the bulbs up and planting them in a temporary six-inch-deep row in the cutting patch, where they will stay until they ripen. Then I shall put them on a rack in the cellar, where they will lie until November.

The first course, then, of a good three weeks' duration, was pink and white. (My pink tulips were Clara Butts, and my white ones Zwanenburgs; both of them fine, tall, long-blooming Darwins.) The second course in this border banquet is really a succession of overlapping dishes, and a very lengthy one, lasting from Decoration Day to Labor Day; and while in those three months it changes character considerably from time to time, it maintains one distinguishing feature, which is its color scheme of blue and white. In striking contrast to the cool serenity of this long summer episode, the dessert will come on after Labor Day with loud cries of chrysanthemums in yellow, red, terra cotta and white.

The blue-and-white season begins with iris and columbine. The iris I used are two old favorite varieties, pallida dalmatica (blue) and White Knight, and the columbines are the blue and white Aquilegia caerulea. Right now these are both at the height of their performance, and it is hard to believe that that best of all possible blue-and-white combinations, Madonna lilies and Belladonna delphiniums, which at any moment now will be dominating the border, can be any more beautiful.

Before the lilies and delphinium have finished, the late summer part of the repast will have come on in the form of phlox, veronica platycodon and babysbreath. And here, of course, the same blue-and-white scheme will prevail, with the pure white phlox Mary Louise; with Veronica longifolia subsessiles (one of the finest perennials); with the large platycodon in both the white and blue varieties; and with gypsophila (babysbreath) Bristol Fairy for its feathery clouds of white.

I am rather pleased with the four perennials I have picked out for July and August—that quartet of phlox, veronica, platycodon and babysbreath. They carry on the blue-and-white arrangement so well. And while I know the gardener will be waiting to fill in a lot of spaces with annuals, I am afraid for once she won't have a chance.

Of course, some of these things will *want* to keep on with a scattered blooming right into September and October, but as fast as they bloom in the fall, all but the phlox will be cut for the house, so they won't interfere with my chrysanthemum scheme.

The chrysanthemums I keep in the cutting patch until August, when, as they are in bud, I transplant them bodily to the border, putting them wherever I find a place, even though it means a little crowding here and there. From my experience with chrysanthemums they don't seem to mind, any more than the tulips, being treated as itinerants; and just before the first heavy freezing —as part of the final cleaning up—I lift them out of the border and put them back in their row in the cutting patch, for division in the spring.

I happen to prefer the single and semi-double varieties of chrysanthemums, and my flamboyant array will be made up of the scarlet Dazzler, the orange-red Shirley Terra Cotta, the bronzy-yellow Alice Howell, the bronze-red and wine-red Korean hybrids Mercury and Mars, and plenty of the pure white Ruth Hatton.

This design for a border banquet seems to me far superior to the hit-or-miss method, such as the gardener was accustomed to use, for all that method's undeniable charm.

Tools and a place for working under cover

The gardener's bench is not a bench, of course, in the sense of a place to sit, but a long firm workable table or counter fastened securely to the wall of the garage, under two north windows.

It is eight feet long, two feet wide and four feet high. There is a low shelf underneath it near the floor, on which we keep a supply of flats for seeds and seedlings, an assortment of pots in various sizes, and a row of boxes containing garden loam, leaf mold, peat moss, sand, and some pebbles for pot-drainage and bulb bowls. Above the bench on shelves and hooks beside the window are plant labels, packages of seeds, a fine sieve, a small watering can with a long spout, a trowel and a little home-made dibble. This collection of tools, equipment and materials is all the gardener needs for raising plants from seed. Her seed flats are only ten inches square, so she plants just one variety of seed to a flat, which simplifies the whole process of cultivation and transplanting. When the time comes for transplanting the seedlings she sets them out in larger flats, where they grow on for potting or for the garden.

The gardener's personal kit is a very compact affair. It consists of her trowel (a straight one with a steel shank), a hazeltine hand weeder, a flower scissors that holds the cut stem, a ball of green twine, some plant labels, and a four-quart watering can with a long spout and a fine nose. Everything but the pot she carries in a flat basket, like a platter, with a high arching handle. The basket comes in handy for cut flowers. She used to wear gloves in the garden, but has given them up in favor of some protective hand lotion she has discovered, and she has also discarded the kneeling pad in favor of a piece of plywood, for days when the ground is damp and cold; though she never kneels long enough now in any one place to make a kneeling-board necessary.

Of course, the gardener's duties are of a nature which makes it possible for her to get along with what would be, for regular garden work, a rather inadequate array of implements. Hers is the hand work, as opposed to the arm and body work that is my particular portion. So it is my tools which occupy most of the wall space on the garden side of the garage.

The principal items in my collection are, needless to say, that time-honored trio, the spade, the rake and the hoe. Some gardeners claim that these three implements are all that a real gardener needs; that all the rest were made for dilettanti. I can't agree with this entirely.

My spade is not actually a spade, but a spading fork. I have a spade which I use for transplanting shrubs and small trees, but for garden work I prefer a fork, and the fork of my choice is an English pattern, an extremely sturdy tool that will stand up against the heaviest kind of soil and all the force you care to place upon it. My favorite garden rake is one of the steel bow type with the teeth curving slightly inward, and my regular garden hoe has a six-inch blade and a socket that fits over the end of the handle like the finger of a glove. These three fine tools perform the most fundamental of all garden operations, and sometimes I see the point of view of the old dirt gardeners who look upon all other tools, in a way, as interlopers.

An interloper of which I am very fond, however, is a combination weeder and cultivator, with three tines below and a blade above, which has an uncanny way of uprooting the weedlets and pulverizing a crusty surface, close to the row and in between the plants, without disturbing even the tender seedlings.

I must admit that I can practice the lighter forms of weeding and cultivating with this implement more easily than I can with the garden hoe, though if I could own no more than one tool in this category I should have to keep the hoe and do without my cultivator.

My group of weeding and cultivating tools also includes a Warren hoe (the heart-shaped variety), a scuffle hoe and a pull hoe. I use them all occasionally; but whether this is just as a change or because in certain circumstances they are actually better, I'm not in a position to say.

When, because of the weather or my own neglect, the weeds have got the better of my garden, none of my tools seems adequate; but in such a moment there are always several tools in the catalogues or in the shops which seem to me then the only way out of my predicament. And sometimes I buy them, if the gardener isn't looking; and in the ecstasy of trying them out I somehow manage to get the weeds under control, after which I carry on with my customary equipment. And so my collection increases.

The task of keeping these tools in condition is, I suppose, more or less a matter of habit. It has something to do with a sense of neatness which, in my case, is sometimes fairly strong and sometimes rather weak.

Each tool has its own special hook on the wall beyond the gardener's bench; and I try to put my tools there whenever I have finished with them in the garden. But now and then at the end of a hot afternoon, try as I will, I can't return them to their places, but lean them carefully against the garden gate instead.

This, of course, is something a tidy gardener would never do, even if he were going to resume his work the next day at dawn. A tidy gardner never leaves his tools out overnight, but cleans them carefully (wipes them off with an oily rag if necessary) and puts them where they belong.

When tools are new, or when they seem to have done their work especially well, and I am not too tired, I invariably polish them off and put them away. And invariably in the process I find that I have to do the same with the gardener's kit as well.

Further consideration of cultivating

We had been away for several weeks one summer when the garden was young, and on our return we found the flowers all interwoven with weeds and the surface of the soil in the beds all caked and crackly, like pictures of the moon. As the gardener couldn't stand the reproachful looks of her plants, and as I was busy right then with other matters, we installed Mr. Butterworth for a few days as gardener's assistant's assistant. Mr. B. was a burden in many ways, but his performance with the hoe was something beautiful to see.

It was a regular garden hoe which he had cut down on the sides until the blade was only about two inches wide. The bottom edge and the right-hand edge he kept very sharp with a file that he carried in the hip pocket of his overalls, together, I am afraid, with a small flask. The blade was so narrow that he could work among the plants in the perennial border without injuring the rightful occupants, yet so keen that he sould reduce the weeds to shreds and mix them with the surface soil which, in the same operation, would be transformed from crust to powder.

It was quite a lesson, and I was sorry to see Mr. Butterworth leave, but the gardener caught him cultivating a poppy into shreds every now and then along with the weeds—whether through fervor or because of the flask we couldn't be sure—and she asked him for his resignation.

We learned about one kind of cultivating from him, but we soon discovered that in other circumstances other techniques were more suitable. For example, there have been occasions right after a long spell of wet weather when the weeds were so large that it would have been next to impossible to follow Mr. B.'s masticating method, even with a hoe like his (which, by the way, is now on the market, known as a narrow hoe). In such a case the topsoil would also be too damp for proper cultivation, but just right for pulling up the weeds easily by hand, roots and all. Pulling from a hard-baked bed is a waste of time, as roots rarely come along.

Weeds, of course, are only one reason for cultivating. The most important reason, because in a way it covers weed control as well, is the keeping of the surface soil of the garden in a loose and pulverized condition. This is not only for the sake of neatness, as the gardener used to think. A fine, loose soil surface prevents the rapid evaporation of moisture from the ground; so effectively, in fact, that really conscientious cultivating obviates the necessity for watering, except during prolonged dry spells. Strange as it may seem, soil moisture evaporates very readily through a tightly packed or crusty surface. And naturally the whole idea is to keep this moisture in the ground, as close to the plant roots as possible.

The proper depth for cultivation in a flower bed is about one inch. Deeper working of the soil is apt to result in damage to the roots; besides, it isn't necessary. For this reason, hoes and other long-handled cultivating tools should be used with considerable care until you have acquired a certain amount of skill. For the flower beds I find the narrow hoe and the three-tined speedy cultivator the safest and most efficient; the former for the tallish weeds and the crusty surface, the latter for weedlings and soft-surface work. The variety of cultivating tools is tremendous, but for me the real value of most of them—the scuffle hoes, pull hoes, and so on—lies in their usefulness in the vegetable-garden rows.

Keeping the garden under control in summer

Somewhere in her kit the gardener always keeps an ounce of prevention. It takes the form of proper watering; of staking and tying tall or weak-stemmed plants; of timely cutting; of fertilizing with foresight; of keeping ahead of the weeds; and of outwitting the pests. And by her prompt attention to these items on the summer garden program she manages our border with a minimum of work—anywhere from a few minutes to an hour in the early morning, and the same at sundown, leaving the garden to its own devices during the heat of the day, which is best for all concerned.

The most important part of the work is the watering, and the most important part of the watering is the way it is done, and when. We practice two kinds of watering in the garden; sprinkling and occasional soaking. The sprinkling is always performed at the evening session, when there is no danger that rapid evaporation will harm the foliage. It is done with a fine spray nozzle on the hose, and done gently but thoroughly, so that the leaves are not merely wet, but washed. This not only freshens the plant but does a lot to discourage insects and diseases.

And we observe this ritual daily, unless of course there has just been rain or we can actually see it coming. Sprinkling dampens the surface of the soil, but doesn't penetrate to the roots, which is where soaking comes in. This is done with the nozzle removed and with an easy flow of water, as any force would do as much damage as good. As a further precaution the gardener sticks the end of the hose in a five-inch flowerpot and lays the pot on its side in a large saucer. The water then spills harmlessly over the rim of the saucer and in the course of a few minutes soaks quite a little area. The saucer, pot and hose are then moved along, and the operation continued until the whole border has been soaked.

There are two watering devices now on the market worth considering, both of which make use of the gentle soaking method. One is a porous hose that can be laid straight along a row or woven through a wider border, and from it water leaks out evenly along its entire

[Continued on page 44]

Wall Garden

A wall garden is a rock garden with a meaning. Not just a random arrangement of stones trying to look like a miniature mountain or quarry, but stones usefully at work, and in whose crevices the proper plants are grown to make the whole affair as beautiful as it is practical—even more so. The stones should be laid with a certain soil mixture between them (instead of mortar) to give the plants their sustenance and to hold the stones in place. The ideal mixture is one third sand and two thirds leaf mold, an inch or more of this between all the stones. And the stones (in walls) should pitch back slightly from the face of the wall, and the face of the wall should also slant back slightly, so the plant roots can catch the rain. Plants can be set in the cracks as the stones are laid, or after, as you wish; that is, if plants are used instead of seeds; and I would recommend plants, if feasible, as they are not expensive, and as many rock-plant seeds, though by no means all, are rather difficult to raise. And if you are tempted by this picture to make a wall garden right away, get in touch at once with a rock-plant specialist who can furnish you not only with proper seeds and plants but with expert advice as to the preparations for growing them in your particular locality. Then, when spring comes, hold your breath!

This wall-garden setting was especially planned to show rock plants as decoration for the simple forms of stone walls and steps. The plants in the picture include:

Gypsophila repens, Creeping Babysbreath; Iberis Little Gem, Candytuft; Sempervivum arachnoideum, Spiderweb Houseleek; Armeria maritima alba, Common Thrift; Veronica teucrium prostrata, Harebell Speedwell; Antennaria dioica, Common Pussytoes; Sedum pruniatum, Forster's Stonecrop; Polemonium reptans, Creeping polemonium; Sempervivum calcareum, Houseleek; Viola Johnny-jump-up; Sedum acre, Goldmoss; Asplenium ebeneum, Ebony Spleenwort; Sempervivum haussmanni, Haussmann's Houseleek; Sempervivum Mayfair hybrid; Phlox subulata, Vivid, Moss Phlox; Seed heads of Anemone pulsatilla, European Pasqueflower; Viola canadensis, Canada Violet; Aquilegia pyrenaica, Columbine; Alyssum saxatile compactum flora plen, Dwarf Goldentuft; Sedum dasyphyllum, Leafy Stonecrop; Thymus serpyllum album, White Mother-of-Thyme; Thymus serpyllum coccineus, Crimson Thyme; Sempervivum tissieri, Houseleek; Prostrate Juniper; Hybrid Azalea.

A SPRING GARDEN CORNER OF RHODODENDRON AND AZALEA

Gardens of azaleas and rhododendrons are so tremendously popular that every spring people by the thousand travel hundreds of miles to be figuratively swept off their feet by famous gardens of azaleas, by mountains melting with rhododendrons in bloom, and by hillsides hidden in white clouds of dogwoods. Yet here is something anyone can witness by walking out into his own garden: azalea, rhododendron, dogwood—not to mention hemlock—all occupying a corner fifteen feet square, and costing whatever you can afford to pay, as determined by how long you are willing to wait. For there are two ways to plant a garden corner of this kind. One is to buy large plants and make an immediate effect, and one is to buy small plants and watch them develop. The latter costs a fraction of the first and, depending upon the size of the plants you decide to buy, may take anywhere from three to five years to reach an appearance of maturity. However, both azaleas and rhododendrons begin to bloom as soon as they come out of the cradle, so the waiting period has its compensations.

Unless you already have ideal conditions for growing these particular plants—that is, a woodsy soil in a spot well sheltered from the wind and somewhat shaded—you must first make thorough preparations as follows: Dig up the bed to a depth of eighteen inches; remove the worst one third of the soil and replace with peat moss or leaf mold. If you can get your hands on a lot of partially rotted oak leaves, you will have one of the best of all ingredients; but avoid anything that smacks of lime—limestone, whitewash, plaster and certain fertilizers—and remember always that these plants just don't like lime. If you happen to live in a limestone region you will have to be careful to keep the soil somewhat acid, with peat moss or leaf mold worked into the bed, with mulches of oak leaves or peat moss, and even with occasional ground dressings of aluminum sulphate.

As for shelter from the prevailing winds, which is just as important as the acidity of the soil, a compact planting of evergreens will work out beautifully—which is the part the hemlocks play in the picture—if there is no building, wall, fence or heavy planting to do the job. Until an adequate windbreak has been developed you will have to provide a winter screen of evergreen boughs or burlap.

Protection from the sun is not of as vital importance, but what is called "passing shade" is decidedly beneficial to all evergreen shrubs. This is the part the dogwood plays in the picture—this and its spring and fall costumes of flower and fruit. But morning shade from any deeprooted tree will answer the sun-protection purpose.

As for the plants themselves—out of one of the largest of all plant families, it is well to use two types of azaleas and one of rhododendron: one is a pink variety of Kurume hybrid azalea; another is the yellow to orange variety of Mollis hybrids. With these the white and pink varieties of Rhododendron carolinianum are appropriate.

For plants of good size you will pay from seventy-five cents up for the Kurumes, from a dollar and a half up for the Mollis, and from one to five dollars up for the Carolina rhododendrons; but if you are willing to play along with "transplants," which are the next stage above seedlings, you can buy them for as little as six for a dollar. These transplants, nursed along under a lath screen, will in no time become large enough to be set out. That will give you plenty of time to learn their habits and requirements, and to get a place ready for them which will be suitable to their dazzling beauty.

length. The other is a four-foot long, light metal nozzle for the end of a regular hose, from whose open end the water comes out in a gentle stream, right at the ground. Of course, the surface of the soil should be loose and open; otherwise, no matter what you use, absorption won't be fast and thorough.

And as a rule we don't try to soak the whole garden on any one evening, but do it in sections at a time. Certain plants, such as tall-bearded iris, we seldom water, as they would much rather not be wet. However, Japanese iris are an exception. They want all the water they can get.

The gardener is a great believer in bone meal, and every few weeks she stirs a trifle into the soil around the plants before she starts the sprinkling. Perhaps she spoils them, but they certainly seem to thrive from this little extra feeding; and when other gardens show the effect of difficult late midsummer days, her border is flourishing. Right now the phlox and babysbreath are white clouds against a blue sky of speedwell and larkspur, and every plant is clean, erect and full of vigor.

There are a few lilies in among the bella donna delphiniums; and because the garden is in a rather windy place, the gardener stakes them as a precautionary measure. As a matter of fact, she stakes the delphiniums too, and even the phlox, although she feels these plants should stand up by themselves. But we've learned from experience that when they are heavy with bloom, they are apt to be bent or broken by a strong breeze. We use thin, green-stained bamboo, which is slender, strong, attractive—and inexpensive.

The gardener cuts the flowers in the cutting patch as soon as they open, and takes them into the house; but in the border, whose purpose is purely decorative, she waits to cut the flowers until they start to fail, which not only keeps up the garden's appearance but in many cases prolongs the blooming period considerably. Delphinium, for instance, when treated this way in late June and early July, responds with a fine crop of flowers again in the fall, and even when cutting in advance of seed formation doesn't result in further flowering, the plant, relieved from the strain of going to seed, keeps in attractive condition longer than it would otherwise.

All these things—watering, staking and cutting—keep the plants in such a healthy, clean and vigorous state that they are seldom bothered by bugs or diseases. But occasionally certain kinds of plants, in spite of constant watchfulness on the part of the gardener, will prove susceptible to the same insect or ailment every season—such as the hollyhock to the Japanese beetle (which is one of the principal pests in our part of the country). Then we simply give up hollyhocks, or whatever else it happens to be, rather than be bothered. If the disease or insect is easy to control, like red spider on the phlox, the gardener takes it in her stride, using one of the prepared combination sprays in her small hand sprayer. But whenever she sprays a plant, she sprays completely, for otherwise it is largely a waste of time.

The little spraying she has to do is done at the early morning session, which is the best time to examine the plants for bugs, mildew, and so on. But the real object of this dawn work is the weeding and cultivating. The soil, from the wetting of the evening before and the dampness of the night is in just the right condition for pulling weeds up easily without leaving the roots in the ground. It is also just right for stirring up with the hand claw or cultivator, crumbling nicely with hardly any effort on the gardener's part, and preventing the formation of a crust, which would surely happen during the day.

These garden hours of hers are well placed for outwitting the heat. Everything is done at a time when it is comparatively cool, leaving practically the whole day free for enjoying the garden in comfort.

Flowers that like it hot and dry

I have in mind the plants in our garden which seem to thrive in the hot spots, the really toasted situations, such as along the top of the low retaining wall and in the two corners of the border called the sun traps. I am sure there are similarly dry and difficult places in almost every garden. It is not much fun to work in those places except at dawn or sundown, so the certain plants that grow there for us have to be able to stand a good deal of neglect. And the ones to which I give honorable mention not only manage to endure the heat and the dryness but actually appear to prefer it.

It is the gardener's opinion that of all these hot-and-dry plants, the palm should go to portulaca. And now that these creeping, intensely floriferous and practically irrepressible little annuals can be grown in segregated colors, and

in single as well as double varieties, I am inclined to agree with her. The flowers that cover the little carpets of succulent foliage are the size of a half dollar, cup-shaped, and of no account for cutting—just a garden decoration. The singles are like buttercups, while the doubles are like little roses. They are very easy to raise from early spring sowings, as soon as the ground is warm.

Against the shed the gardener has another long, narrow bed that gets rather ovenlike by midday in August. What she has done there may be looked at askance by many gardeners, but it is literally a mass of bloom from June until frost, and never more luxuriant than during the dog days. The bed is not much more than two feet wide, and t the back, against the whitewashed building, is a row of pink geraniums. In front of the geraniums is a row of heliotrope, and in front of the heliotrope a row of ageratum. This descending scale of pink, purple and lavender-blue is then garnished along the forward edge of the bed with an irregular ribbon of single white portulaca. The whole effect is as old-fashioned as a horsehair sofa, and the pungent sweet fragrance, especially in the heat, is full of spicy perfume.

In the two sun-trap corners of the border, where the composition calls for something tall that will flower white, we have set a plant apiece of Spanish bayonet—the old reliable Yucca filamentosa. On the four-foot stems that tower above the sharp spiky leaves are great bouquets of pure white bells, while setting them off at a slightly lower level are the flaming yellow flowers of Argemone, or prickly poppy—one of the finest of all large, hot-weather annuals.

The yucca is, of course, a perfectly hardy perennial.

Elsewhere in the full sun of the garden are three August-blooming varieties of Hemerocallis, golden yellow, permanent and prolific. The gardener has been somewhat slow to give these more and more popular day lilies her blessing, probably because they require so little of her tender care, but now she is no longer able to resist their charms.

Keeping up with the Iris

A few years ago the gardener, who rarely reads garden books, picked up an unusually nourishing morsel by John C. Wister, called "The Iris," which she devoured in forty-five minutes. And as a result, from having merely dabbled in irises, we now wallow in them, and spend almost a week in August dividing the clumps that a few years back we planted as single roots, or rhizomes, as they are called. These divisions we then replant—at least, as many as we have room for; the rest we give away.

For the iris—at any rate, the tall, bearded type—is for the most part a plant that multiplies with great rapidity. A single rhizome, in several seasons, becomes quite a cluster of roots; and to keep the plant in healthy condition and the flowers at full size, it is essential every five years, more or less, to cut and wrench the clump apart, reducing it again to single rhizomes.

We don't try to divide all our irises at one time, but take a different section every year. And we don't always make the entire annual division in August, though we have come to consider that a very satisfactory season for the job. As a matter of fact, we have had the best results from dividing irises on the Fourth of July after they have finished flowering; and we have also done it in early fall. For in June there is too much going on; and by planting in the fall there is just a chance that the roots won't get firmly established before winter sets in and will be heaved out by the frost. This actually happened with us last winter, and the gardener was horrified in March to find practically all the roots she had so carefully planted in late October lying loosely on the surface of the ground. She was even more horrified when I casually firmed them in with my foot, and she greeted their growing in May with great astonishment. She should have known that an iris will stand for almost anything.

When it comes to dividing, I perform the first operations—lift the clump with a spade, slice it through from the top once or twice with the sharp edge of the same implement, then pull the rhizomes partly apart. After which the gardener takes the broken clump, snips all but three inches of the leaves off with a pair of long scissors, separates the individual rhizomes and throws them in a garden basket for planting. And by the time I have prepared the ground, by loosening and pulverizing it as deeply as I can with a mattock, and mixing in the bone meal (a pound to every twelve plants when set a little more than a foot apart) the planting is practically nothing. A stroke of the trowel makes room for the roots, which hang down from the rhizome, when firmed in, just about half covered. We keep the soil around the roots fairly moist for two weeks after planting, then never bother to water them again.

Iris raising can soon become a cult, what with all the new varieties offered each year; but we have stuck to the older, less expensive kinds, and are very happy with them. Our favorites are Fairy and Ma Mie for white effects; the fine old lavender Princess Beatrice; the deep purple Souvenir de Mme. Gaudichau (pronounced "go-de-show"), and the pure, rich yellow Shekinah. These are all beautiful in the big bold masses where irises, in my opinion, belong, but the gardener has used the more unusual colors, and combinations of colors, very effectively among her other flowers. The choice is wide enough to satisfy any taste.

Lawn-conscious

The gardener has always taken grass for granted, like electricity or running water. As long as the lawn looked all right, she never took an active part in its physical welfare—just enjoyed it as part of the general background. Occasionally she would comment on the fact that it needed cutting, but I really believe this was an unconscious habit, too, or mental telepathy; for she invariably mentioned the mowing at the moment I was about to do it anyhow.

Within the last week or so, however, she has not only become aware of the lawn, but has assumed a rather critical attitude toward my management of it. And I must say there is some occasion for her concern, though the condition of the lawn is not altogether due to my neglect. The moles, for instance, were not my fault.

These blind rodents had never been here before, and I don't think they enjoyed their first visit very much. The morning I saw those two long winding ridges across the lawn, I planted red pepper in small holes along the tracks and waited to see what would happen. What happened was another welt the next morning. I gave this track the same treatment, and for the next few days there was nothing new. Then one evening I noticed a slight activity of the turf near the end of a track, hurried for a spade, dug it down in front of the movement and quickly pried up a piece of sod, and with it a mole—a foolish-looking animal with nice fur. It was the last one we had. I like to think they left on account of the pepper, as I don't like poisons, and the gardener doesn't like traps.

I suppose that couldn't be called a bad attack of moles. There wasn't any need to try traps, or the poison-bait treatment either. The pepper worked very well, and I shall have it ready for them if they ever decide to come back. In the meantime I've tamped the soil back level along the little ridges, and at least for a while we can consider the mole episode at an end.

Unfortunately, there are still the brown spots in the lawn where the beetle grubs ate the grass-roots. The good grass is dead in these scattered areas, but the tall, unattractive tufts of crab grass are coming along fine, as they have an irritating way of lying down in front of the mower and then springing right back erect as soon as the mower has passed.

What I'm doing here in these unhappy places is to stir the patches with a rake, and spread on a good complete fertilizer that I water in. Then when the ground is dry I rake it again to a fine finish, spread on a generous quantity of the best grass-seed mixture I can buy, run the rake over it lightly, roll it with an empty roller, and sprinkle it gently every evening.

A small spreader is a splendid and inexpensive piece of equipment for anyone with a lawn. It make a very simple matter of both fertilizing and seeding; and by making it possible to fertilize and seed evenly and in just the proper amount, it saves enough in a season or two to pay for itself. I have always found it difficult to gauge the right amount of grass seed or fertilizer to use when the directions say seven hundred pounds to the acre, or even when they say one pound to a hundred square feet. A little lever on the spreader settles this question once and for all. All you do is fill the hopper, set the lever, and push the spreader along as you would a lawn mower—only it is much easier.

I've learned not to use lime on the lawn, because I'm convinced, rightly or wrongly, that it encourages the crab grass. And I've learned not to use ordinary manure, because there is no doubt at all that it brings in weeds. The best thing for a lawn, of course, is plenty of humus, but the most rapid-acting applications are fertilizers and if they are put on properly, and the soil is right, the grass will get so vigorous that weeds won't have a chance.

I like to make my major lawn maneuvers at the end of August. That was when I made the lawn originally, and the grass got under way so well that I could have mowed it before the end of the season. As early as possible in the spring I rake it over thoroughly and give it fertilizer. Then in June, right after a mowing—and right before a rain

if it can be managed—I spread bone meal at the rate of two pounds to a hundred square feet, according to the lever. From the middle of May to the middle of September I keep the lawn mower set rather high—two inches—so that the roots won't be bothered by the heat, and I leave the grass cuttings alone to act as a mulch, unless they're long enough to mat down on the turf.

The last week in August, right after a mowing and just before a rain if possible, I rake the lawn thoroughly, clean out any crab grass that may have crept in, spread on a complete fertilizer, seed any poor patches that may have developed, and give it a good rolling. Sometimes, in a fit of extravagance, I spread a thin sowing of grass seed over the whole lawn; and I can recommend a similar indulgence to anyone whose lawn is not the last word in luxuriance. The final work on the lawn comes when the mowing is over for the season, when I spread—by hand and rake—about a quarter-inch of humus, preceded by a final application of bone meal.

The result is certainly worth the effort. I know it took two seasons of no treatment at all—just mowing and watering—for my lawn to degenerate. And even then it wasn't so bad as the gardener made it sound. It was really the moles that made her think about the grass, then noticed the rest.

The gardener on the warpath

The gardener's fierceness toward the various pests developed rather gradually. In fact, at first she was inclined to

[Continued on page 53]

Garden Without Flowers

This garden speaks entirely in the language of leaves. Many gardeners, on the other hand, may find it sufficient merely to intersperse a few items of colorful foliage among their flowers. Other may care to go further. In any event, this especially designed setting will serve as a little dictionary for anyone with a taste for something different.

First of all, the wall, which is laid up of hollow cinder blocks, whitewashed, is there to protect the tenderish caladiums from the wind, and to furnish a unique planting place, in its soil-filled cavities, for a living top of striped-leaved peperomias and wandering-jew.

The tubers of the bright-leaved caladiums, as well as the elephant's ears, can be planted as soon as warm weather comes, but must be taken up before frost and stored over winter, like gladiolus. The plants of the peperomias and wandering-jew, from the florist, can be potted up in the fall and used until spring for indoor decoration.

The most important, varied and brilliant of the foliage plants, coleus, has been rather neglected ever since the days when it was so badly abused as a bedding plant—on station banks especially—much to the disadvantage of gardening. It is absurdly easy to raise either from seed or cuttings; and when from seed, the results are a constant and colorful surprise. You may have to experiment with coleus to find the ones which perform best in your garden; after which it is a simple matter to perpetuate your favorites with cuttings.

A good peaty soil, plenty of watering, protection from exposure for all but the coleus, which aren't particular, and you will discover that in addition to the fact that you can say it with flowers—as everyone knows—you can say it with foliage too.

Caladiums are against the bottom of the wall, wandering-jew in the hollow piers, and peperomias as a live coping. Elephant's ears, or colocasias, build up a bold background, while everything else is vari-colored coleus.

treat them tenderly, if not to disregard them entirely. But as she became aware of the damage they were doing, as her fondness for her plants increased, as she got to know her garden better, she saw the havoc wrought by the cutworms, the borers, the aphids, the beetles, and she flew to the defense of her flowers.

Her principal weapons are a small sprayer and a small duster. Their smallness was my suggestion. I knew from experience that anything heavy and hard to handle would only defeat its purpose by discouraging the gardener from using it as often as she should. I believe in garden implements for women which don't impose an unnecessary burden. Lady gardeners do more when they have just the right, light utensil.

Both sprayer and duster work with a plunger, like a bicycle pump. The sprayer has a glass pint jar attached by a screw top, which holds the spray mixture; the duster has a chamber that holds about a pound of dust. In using either weapon, the idea is to give the foliage an *even*, not a *heavy*, coating, underneath as well as above. It took the gardener some time to develop the technique that is now so fatal to her prey.

The fatal materials she prefers are of two kinds, though both kinds are harmless to humans and to humans' pets. One is a liquid spray that comes in highly concentrated form, and which, when diluted to the proper degree for the specific pest as indicated on the container, we have found effective against most insects that annoy the gardener's plants. The other is a dry mixture of dusting sulphur and nicotine which the gardener dusts on her lilacs and phlox to prevent mildew, and on many other plants which are susceptible to red mite. The complete spray, for fighting both sucking and chewing insects, should be obtainable, in various formulas, in any good garden department.

The gardener has a feeling about poisonous sprays, such as ones containing Paris green or arsenate of lead, which may not be altogether justified. The poisonous ones are cheaper and generally more potent, but the gardener would rather spray more expensively and oftener than place her kittens in jeopardy. And as the various beetles are the most difficult insects to kill, with or without poison, she has steeled herself to remove them by hand, by picking or flicking or shaking them off and depositing them in a can containing an inch or two of kerosene, where they expire.

Plant pests and their control, not to mention plant diseases and *their* control, must seem bewildering matters to many beginners. The gardener could never make head or tail of the more serious treatises on the subject; has learned all she knows from actual observation and from the directions that come with the various sprays. In fact, all she brought away from the books was the part about parasites. She learned that the ladybug (fly away home) and the fearful-looking praying mantis are insects to encourage, as they live on the harmful insects and do no harm themselves. She collects all the ladybugs she can and brings them to the garden, but lets the praying mantises come of their own free will and understandably, in case you've ever seen one.

A time for relaxation

By the time her hardy phlox has all come out like a chorus in calico, the gardener is ready to relax. Mid-July marks the summit of her working season, and from this point on through the heat of August she does all the coasting she can. As far as she is concerned, Nature needs no further encouragement now.

What she does about that comes, for her, under the head of relaxation, it being mostly a matter of scissors, and no stooping or kneeling to speak of. Work, in her estimation, is getting down with a trowel or with her miniature spade and hoe, and having to wear gloves. Simply to go through the garden at sunset, keeping her plants in check with bare hands and bright blades, is her notion of nothing at all. And so it seems to me, too, as I lug the watering can back and forth and do my best to discourage the weeds.

However, it is just as important as the heavier work I have to do, and to my taste a lot more tedious. For removing the flowers as they fade, thus preventing them from going to seed— though it would seem a monotonous undertaking to me—does definitely prolong the blooming season of the plants by conserving their energy. Also, there is no doubt that it keeps the garden looking neater, which makes the task, already entertaining to the gardener, profoundly satisfying as well.

It is amazing how many weeks of flowering it adds to the hardy phlox alone, this keeping the fading heads cut. And one of the worst features of phlox is circumvented in the process. For many novices have come to believe that phlox

plants revert in time of their own accord to an undesirable magenta, which is not the case. It is the phlox seeds that fall to the ground which cause the trouble. Phlox varieties almost invariably come wrong from seed, only true from cuttings. The original plant never changes its color.

The gardener's plants rarely reach the point of having to have their seed pods removed, the spent flowers seldom eluding her long enough to form fruit. Which is only one reason for her constant cutting. Another reason is to remove stems and stalks, as well as flowers, which are pest-ridden or diseased, and which are then promptly turned over to me for burning.

The gardener moves along the beds with scissors in hand and two flat baskets beside her. One basket for faded and affected flowers, stems and stalks; one for flowers for the house. Most of the latter come from a bed devoted primarily to cutting, but even among the "show" beds there are occasional perfect blooms, suitable for indoor decoration, whose removal might improve the appearance of the border.

These deep-summer activities of the gardener's come under the head of what she calls relaxation—and I really believe she considers them to be just that. August is a good time for gardeners to relax, if they can. It's a good time to do their gardening in the twilight. And it's a good time at least to limit themselves, like the gardener, to gardening in its milder forms. The kind of relaxing she does is the type of attention the garden would ask for during these warmest weeks of the year, if it could talk.

Exceptions prove the garden rule

When the gardener first began to garden, she planted according to a pair of very simple rules. No. 1 was for her to sow all her seeds as early in the spring as I could get the ground in shape. And No. 2 was not to let me move anything with roots until the fall. Of course, that was too few rules, she knows by now, to cover the many complexities of planting; and in addition, the rules themselves were far too simple. But they were just right for her at the time.

And now I sometime sigh for those delightful days, when everything was so nice and elementary and there was nothing to do from May till October but weed and spray and cultivate and water. For the gardener has grown garden-wise, and there's not a month in the year when she's not apt to sow some seeds—or plant some plants, as far as that goes.

For example, ever since June, off and on, she has been lifting our few oversized clumps of iris, dividing the roots and replanting them—an operation she'd never have countenanced in the early days, until the iris leaves had begun to wither in September, indicating approaching dormancy. She still considers the fall-planting rule theoretically sound; as plants whose growth naturally slackens in the later season are less inclined to suffer then from transplanting. But she found the iris didn't object to this disturbance in summer, and when well watered in actually preferred it, for they then had a chance to become root-anchored before alter-nating frost and thaw had a chance to heave them loose.

She also found that peonies, as well as Oriental poppies, could be transplanted as early as shortly before Labor Day without any subsequent harm; which was quite at variance with her original notion. And as for day lilies (*Hemerocallis*), she has now become so bold as to move them in full bloom. Which is something of a boon, for while these plants can go ten years without dividing, it is pleasant to know that such a golden fountain can be transferred to a more effective spot on the spur of the moment. She has even begun to trade full-grown day lilies, in flower, with her neighbors—one variety for another, and no chance of error.

As a matter of fact, carrying out an arrangement of the gardener's with a friend of hers, I trundled one of our huge clumps of the purple iris, Madame Gaurichau, down the road in the wheelbarrow, and brought back an equally large clump of the yellow iris Helios, of which we had none. That was about the first of June, and both clumps were in full flower; but they went right on blooming as though nothing had happened.

So while it was no doubt a good thing for the gardener to have begun with but two rules, and those extremely conservative, I must admit that gardening for her has become a more satisfying occupation now that she has learned some of the many exceptions. She no longer waits till spring to sow certain annual seeds, like cornflower, Shirley poppy and larkspur, but occasionally sows them in the fall, where they're to grow; and the next year reaps a really bountiful, long and early crop of bloom.

Getting a few shrubs
in the ground

We have just been planting a few more shrubs. A pair of bush arbutus (Abelia grandiflora) —one on either side of the garden gate; a cluster of four for-sythia at the corner of the lawn; two maple-leaf viburnums on the shady side of the house, a witch-hazel bush outside the living room window; where we can watch it flower in February, and a mountain ash, which isn't a shrub, but a flowering tree already ten feet tall.

In the morning I marked the places where they were to go and began dig-ging the holes. I looked at the roots of the mountain ash, which had a spread of about three feet, and marked out a hole four feet in diameter, to make it roomy for the root system. From the ground line on the trunk to the bottom of the roots was about eighteen inches, so I figured on making the hole a little over two feet deep. This extra-size hole would give the new roots a chance to spread themselves in well-prepared loam, and not have to fight through solid earth.

I took a piece of burlap and laid it on the lawn beside the spot where I was going to make the hole for the mountain ash. This was to keep the lawn clean and make the work easier. With a long-handled digging shovel I cut the sod from the three-foot circle and put it on the burlap, giving each piece of sod a few slaps with the shovel blade to break it up. The next eight inches down were good topsoil. Then I struck the subsoil, but a light garden mattock loosened up the shale and clay, and the shovel lifted it onto the burlap, but on another pile.

When the gardener came out I took the mountain ash, trimmed the roots back about one-third with the pruning-shears, did the same to the top, threw about six inches of good topsoil into the bottom of the hole, and tramped it down firmly so that it wouldn't sink away from the roots and leave air pock-ets. Then I set the tree in the hole, gave it to the gardener to hold, and spread the roots out carefully. The first six or eight shovelfuls of soil, from the good pile, I sifted on slowly, letting it fall into all the interstices among the roots, and giving the tree a little per-pendicular shake to help accomplish this very particular part of the planting process. When the roots were practi-cally out of sight I threw in the broken sods and tramped them down. This brought the filling-in to within a couple of inches of the top, and the tree was set firmly enough to stand by itself. So the gardener let go and I filled the de-pression around the tree with water, then filled it up level with the lawn with some of the poor soil from the burlap.

The shubs went much faster, being tiny by comparison with the mountain ash; but the process was practically the same. I did slip in one additional op-eration, much to the gardener's disgust. I muddled them. That is, I brought out a bucket, filled it half full of water, and stirred in fine topsoil until it made a thick brown soup; then into this I dip-ped the roots of each shrub before plant-ing it. This gave the fine rootlets some-thing easy to feed on while they were getting established in their new home.

After the first hard frost, one of us will set a mulch of leaves or salt hay around all the shrubs to keep them from being heaved by alternate freezing and thawing during the winter. Then all through next season we shall keep them well cultivated and watered, and the chances are we won't lose a single plant.

The shrubs aren't much to look at now, but the witch hazel will be sure to bloom in February or March. The forsythia is the finest of all forsythias (*Forsythia intermedia spectabilis*), so I am counting on a golden special display. The viburnums are the variety acerifolium (maple-leaf), and will have white flowers in May and June and be full of black berries in the fall. Also, they will thrive in the shade. The abelia should be practically evergreen and will be filled with pink flowers from June until frost. The mountain ash flowers white in the spring, and bears fine clusters of orange-red berries through the fall.

Cutting and arrangement in simplest form

I don't believe the gardener has ever bothered her head very much about the art of fixing up flowers. She brings them in by the basketfull, or by the bunch, but mostly in a bucket; gets all her receptacles together on the sink; and after a lot of slashing and splashing, I am putting the filled-up vases where they belong, while she goes aroung giving the stems a shake, a pull, a push, the way a woman gives a quick fluff to a curtain. And before you can say Constance Spry the house is beautiful, and the gardener is lying down on the sofa looking at it, and I am wondering which one of us is going to clean up that mess in the pantry.

The main thing for her is to make them last. She starts right off with that

in mind, by making a long slanting slice across the stem as she cuts the flower in the garden. That's to give the amputated stem cells a better chance to function than when they're cut across at right angles.

The gardener is also very particular to make the cut absolutely clean. You can try for yourself, with two cut flowers from the same plant; one broken off and the other sliced off clean with a blade as sharp as a razor. In fact, a razor blade is what the gardener uses, fixed in a handle. She also uses two hands; one to hold the stem and one to cut with. The gardener won't use any of the pruning scissors I've given her— at least not for cutting flowers. You can get a good slanting slice across the stem with a pair of fine, keen pruning scissors, but not so easily, the gardener thinks, as with a razor blade on a handle.

As soon as the flower is cut, the gardener plunges the stem in the bucket of water to keep all stems ends immersed.

Sometimes, when the gardener gets the flowers in the pantry she'll plunge the ends in boiling water for a minute. She's not exactly sure what this does to the stem structure, but she knows it makes the flowers stay fresh much longer. Also, she knows the steam will black the blossoms if it hits them.

She prefers to do her picking just before sundown, though it doesn't always work out that way; but if she does, she leaves the flowers, deep in water, in a cool place all night, and where the sun won't strike them in the morning. Then after breakfast she gets to work on them.

Another thing she does to make them keep is to put a little hydrozenesulphate solution in the vase water. She keeps a bottle of the solution on hand all the time; one ounce of the chemical to a quart of water, and she puts a quarter cup of this into a twelve-quart pailful of the water she uses in the vases. It's worth it, if a day and a half more freshness is of sufficient consequence. Aspirin is easier, and the gardener says it is very good for dahlias.

As for trying to cut the stems off under water, she doesn't think that makes much difference. Just take the flowers out of the water and cut them off where you can get at them easily. This easier way gives you a chance to change the water, which is definitely worth while. And it is likewise worth while, she claims, to take off all leaves below the water line; and some above the water line, too, if the flower stem is a very leafy one, like zinnias.

When it comes to vases, she likes them to have a broad base for solidity, and she likes them to be large enough for a big bouquet. Her favorite vases are those old-fashioned cooky jars of brown or gray pottery, and those big square glass jars that used to be wet-cell storage batteries. For holding flowers in bowls she has an assortment of flower holders of all kinds—not of all kinds, maybe, because there's a new kind every time you turn around; and if she runs out of regular ones she can always make one out of a crumpled handful of poultry wire, which works very well.

Warm weather techniques

From July till September the gardener leaves up the window shade so the morning sun will shine in her face and she will rise to get her gardening in ahead of the heat. Without dwelling on the comparative coolness of early morning, the fragrant freshness and the glittering dew, she can tell you that gardening this soon ofter sunrise has certain other advantages of a practical nature. The soil seems to crumble more readily; the weeds offer less resistance; it's a most effective time for spraying, and the low-angled sunlight brings every plant into such sharp relief that the gardener can quickly see what it wants, if anything.

First of all she gives the ground a good going over; opening its pores, as it were, and whisking out the weeds in the process—not trying to do the whole garden in a single session, but making a thorough job of as much as she can accomplish in comfort. For there's a morning every day, and a clean cultivation lasts a couple of weeks.

A little cultivation, then, and after that a cleaning out of wilted flowers, seed pods, weak stems and infected foliage. These removals not only give the plant more blooming strength, but in their total effect they add immeasurably to the garden's appearance.

I should have said that in the process of cultivating, the gardener scratches in, every two weeks or so, a tablespoonful of complete fertilizer around each one of the plants whose work is not over. Right now, for instance, the tall hardy phlox are the headline feature, and the gardener gives them a little extra food—and waters them daily at the roots. She has fine clumps of Daily Sketch, with its large pink florets; of the dark red Leo Schlageter, and a great deal of the white Miss Lingard whose main blooming time is June, but which keeps on coming out till frost, making it what the gardener considers one of the best behaved of all her hardy plants.

Nothing, she feels, is more deserving of her solicitude throughout these midsummer weeks than those fine phlox, and nothing shows its gratitude more wonderfully for the daily watering and the weekly feeding. In addition she dusts the dewy foliage with powdered sulphur once a week to ward off mildew.

Every week or so, on a morning when the weather forecast is "fair," the gardener does nothing but go over the garden with a good all-purpose spray, giving the foliage a thorough drenching above and below. She doesn't wait for signs of insects or disease; she just goes ahead regardless. The constant cleaning out of crowded stems, spent flowers and withered foliage is, of course, part of this horticultural hygiene; just as a lot of her plant health is due to her clean cultivation.

She keeps a bundle of four-foot bamboo stakes handy, and a hank of raffia, for anything on a single stem that needs support. For plants that are inclined to be floppy, like the tall hardy asters and the big fall cosmos, she provides pieces of branchy brush, rather than have them sprawl down over everything in front.

And all the empty places, like those made by disappearing poppies and bleeding heart, she fills with chrysanthemum plants from the reserve bed, which were divided from the parent stock in the spring. But this operation she performs in the evening, at watering time, so the transplants will have a night in which to recover—and so she will have something new to look forward to in the morning.

Plants that like to stay put

The gardener keeps on remodeling her flower beds, the way other people can't help changing furniture around and switching pictures. For there are certain flowers that turn out to be too tall down front, and others that become too spreading for the space she gave them. Then, of course, there are the plants that like to be taken up periodically and divided, like chrysanthemums every spring and like iris and phlox every three or four years; all further excuses for rearrangement.

In other words, there are many legitimate reasons why flower beds of either annuals or perennials, or both, needn't remain immovable—apart from the fact that it is more fun to keep on doing something different. It's not only to rectify mistakes; it's to satisfy that fundamental craving for change with which most gardeners are afflicted.

But in the gardener's flower beds there are certain plants that remain, like monuments, right where they were planted. Among the most immovable of these is the one the gardener calls fraxinella, which goes under the rather unpleasant name of gas plant, and is known horticulturally as Dictamnus albus. I agree with the gardener that it is one of the best of all perennials. The thing is to get two-year-old seedlings for early-fall or spring planting, and in a year they will begin to bloom; the plants eventually becoming about three feet high and wide—a mass of beautiful foliage from spring to fall, with a splendid array of white summer flowers springing from the top. The leaves and flowers are lemon-scented, and on a still summer evening, if you hold a match to a clustered stem it will give off a flash of light—hence the name gas plant, I suppose. But if you want it to prosper, plant it where it is going to stay. I've seen plants of it that have lived through three generations of gardeners, and are still going strong; no dividing—nothing.

Another plant for garden stability is the old-fashioned favorite, bleeding heart, or Dicentra spectabilis. After its lovely arching flower clusters in the spring, its foliage makes it a mound of beauty until late summer, if the roots are kept well watered; then the plant disappears until spring. But it will keep coming up forever, as far as I know, growing more wonderful every year, if you don't disturb it.

I suppose you can move it if you want. You can even move Dictamnus, as far as that's concerned; only it won't help them any—and as I keep telling the gardener, you've got to have *something* that stays put. So if you're going to get some young bleeding-heart roots, set them out in September in good rich soil, preferably in semi-shade, and where they won't suffer from lack of moisture; then leave them alone as a permanent fixture among your flowers.

Maybe the best of all the permanent perenials is the peony. Anyhow, for the gardener and myself, it completes this triumvirate of perpetual plants for the flower bed. More readily than the bleeding heart and fraxinella, it can be divided from time to time if it gets too large or you want more plants; but instead of cutting up a large old cluster of peony roots into sections each with a single "eye" or stem sprout, the gardener merely makes two or three good-sized clumps of roots out of an ancient plant. Each clump, in this case,

makes a decent peony plant the next spring, if planted by the middle of September, in deep rich soil. Whereas a single-eyed root may take a year or two.

As for varieties, the gardener swears by the red flecked, white Festiva Maxima, the pink Alice Harding, and the dark red Philippe Rivoire—a trio hard to match, like the everlasting fraxinella, bleeding heart and peony themselves.

A few more fertilizers

When she began, the gardener used to treat the soil like dirt. In her flower beds it was the heavy clay kind with which almost everyone is familiar. You had to pound every spadeful to pieces as you dug it up in the spring, and in the summer you had to keep crumbling up the leathery crust that formed as soon as the surface dried off after a rain. But she took the ground as it was for granted, manipulated it the hard way —and things grew, but only after a fashion.

Any gardener likes to grow things better. And this one soon found that her heavy soil was holding her back. The fine roots of annuals couldn't forage for their food, and even the more determined and patient roots of perenials had a pretty hard time. In addition, the fertilizer she scratched into the surface of the ground never seemed to be very effective, even discounting the promises on the package.

To make a long story short, it wasn't until she had put her soil in proper shape that she was able to provide a suitable diet for her plants. She lightened it by digging in coal ashes and sand. This made it possible for water

[Continued on page 64]

Beautiful for a Day

•

Daylilies should certainly be one of the most popular plants in the garden. Anybody can grow them anywhere. They seem to be immune from disease and to have no enemies among the insects. And as for their beauty, I leave that to Mr. Steichen's photograph. They are not true lilies, but belong to the genus Hemerocallis, which is a Greek word meaning "beautiful for a day." The individual blooms generally last from twelve to twenty-four hours, but a well-established plant of Hemerocallis keeps on pouring forth its flowers in great profusion for weeks. Early varieties begin to bloom in May and late ones last into the fall. The colors range from pale lemon yellow to deep ruddy orange, some new hybrids almost red. Daylily roots would probably say they prefer being set out in the early spring, but I have done it at every season except the dead of winter and it didn't seem to make any difference. Three of the original species—flava, thunbergii and fulva—will run the season through and are cheap. The hybrids, of which those illustrated here suggest the color range, are more expensive but are undeniably lovelier. Daylilies multiply with great rapidity and improve with age. They grow on you in more ways than one.

By choosing varieties carefully from any comprehensive catalogue of hemerocallis, or, better yet, by visiting the planting field of any large grower of daylilies and making your selections on the spot, it would be possible to make an entire border of nothing but these plants. There would be fine variety of color from month to month; there is a good range of sizes from one foot high to easily four, and the foliage, before and after flowering, has a long season of attractiveness.

to permeate. Then, to make it capable of absorbing moisture and retaining this moisture in a healthy fashion, she worked in as much leaf mold and pleat moss as she could find and afford. The result eventually was a good crumbly loam, somewhat on the heavy side, but still a loam that wouldn't pack or form a crust. If you filled a Mason jar with it, and poured a little water on the top, you'd see the moisture quickly and evenly finding its way through the entire contents of the glass receptacle, something that would never have happened with the dirt in its original condition. Of course, if her soil had been sandy, which she thinks she'd have preferred, the leaf mold and peat moss would have given it the proper consistency.

For the feeding she gives her garden every six weeks or so during the season, she uses one of the complete, prepared plant foods which contain the various essential nutritious elements required by growing plants. These come in three forms: powder, tablets and liquid. The powdered form she sprinkles lightly around the plant or along the row, scratches it into the surface of the soil, and waters it in.

The tablet form she thrusts several inches into the ground near the plant, then waters. Or if it is a potted plant, she breaks the tablet in half and pushes the piece down along the inside of the pot, from where, as it it dissolves, its nutritious elements are released among the roots.

The concentrated liquid form, which looks like water and is odorless, she dilutes to the proper strength for the maturity of the plants to be fed, soaks the ground around the plant, then waters even that liquid application down into the soil where the roots are waiting for it.

Which form does she prefer? I don't know. She uses all three according to her mood. But the thing that for her is much more important than the type of plant food is the physical condition of her garden soil. The most beautifully balanced meal in the world isn't going to help very much if it can't be digested.

Twilight gardening

If the gardener loses any sleep over her plants in the summer, it's not because she worries about their welfare, but only because she gets up to tend them so early in the morning. She has a theory that they shouldn't be bothered in the heat of the day, but should merely be enjoyed then with as little effort as possible. So any weeding, cultivating or spraying there is to do, she does after the sun goes down. This routine of hers I may have mentioned before, but the plants thrive under it so well I can't help repeating.

Take the dubiously pleasant summer pursuit of spraying, which the gardener despises. In the cool of the morning the mist of the spray—or the dust, if you're dusting—takes hold more evenly when the leaves are still damp with dew; and there also is less danger of burning the foliage. And if it's insects she's after, the gardener has an idea, which may be correct, that at such an early hour they're still too sleepy to escape. It is certainly true of beetles at dawn, and at sundown as well. And though she doesn't relish spraying, I must say the gardener does it thoroughly. With her little plunger spray gun she gets at the underside of the leaves escpecially, as that is where most of the trouble lurks. She uses a liquid spray altogether; not because a dust isn't just as good in many cases—it's merely a personal preference. It's an all-purpose spray, that attacks not only both chewing and sucking insects but fungus diseases as well. And she goes through the garden with it once a week, regardless; which is one reason why she doesn't have to worry much about her plants.

Another reason why she doesn't have to worry much about them is that in her dawn patrol she loosens up the surface of the soil with both a long-handled three-prong cultivator and a short-handled tool of the same type. This careful and constant cultivation keeps the surface of the soil in that desirable crumbly condition which does so much to preserve sub-surface moisture as well as facilitate the penetration of moisture from the hose and the heavens.

The gardener in this early session also attends to whatever staking may be necessary; for which she uses a new type of very soft metal tie-on strip that makes staking, for once, a pleasure. While under sprawly plants, like baby'sbreath and certain asters and chrysanthemums, she pokes a twiggy piece of brush, which forms an ideal support. Needless to say, she also thins out the branches in overcrowded sections of the flower bed and removes all spent blossoms before they have a chance to go to seed.

As a result, the garden looks rejuvenated every day. For in addition to this morning ritual, the gardener performs a ceremony at sundown. This is when she does her watering and cutting—simultaneously. While the water from the hoze with the nozzle removed is gently flowing onto one section of the bed, she is nearby with a pair of sharp snippers, or a razor blade in a handle, getting flowers for the house. By the time her hand is full, the ground is well soaked in one spot; she moves the hose along, and gets back to her cutting. She wets only the ground, never the foliage; and the flowers she puts in a pail of water for the night, to be fixed the next morning.

A cup of autumn crocus

In deepest August, as if in late afternoon, the gardener and her garden need reviving; and it is then that colchicum and autumn crocus come in like a cup of tea. As far as appearances go, they have no business blooming at the end of summer. Their sudden, fragile flowers, starting up from the soil like mushrooms, have all the earmarks of spring; and it's a good plan to put them where they won't look out of place. The gardener plants them in a patch of repeaters that include the creeping Phlox subulata Autumn Rose and iris Eleanor Roosevelt, both of which bloom in the fall as well as the spring. This little bed in September would be like a moment in May if the chrysanthemums crowding in from behind didn't tell an entirely different story.

When the gardener came back from the seed store with her first small bag of colchicum bulbs, she gasped as she poured them out on the table. Two of them had burst into full bloom on the way home. As a matter of fact, some people simply put the bulbs in a bowl dry—no water, dirt or anything—and their flowers come right on out, as if by magic. This, of course, is a characteristic of many bulbs in the lily and iris tribes; the energy for one flowering, at least, being self-contained. I prefer to grow them in the ground—the gardener does too.

Well, for this springlike interlude in early fall there are these two things particularly: *Colchicum autumnale* and *Crocus sativus*. Even the catalogues are inclined to call them both autumn crocuses, and it is true the flowers do look alike, though the plants aren't botanically related in any way. Colchicum bulbs are quite a little larger than crocus bulbs, and a lot more expensive; but once planted, the former live right on and multiply for many years, whereas the latter rarely last for more than a season or two. Colchicum flowers are purple or white: *Crocus sativas,* white or lilac. The colchicum bulbs you plant two to three inches deep, the crocus bulbs three to four. And if you want to know why I don't say exactly two, or three, or four, it's because I've caught the gardener wasting a lot of time carefully measuring depths with a ruler, after reading instructions that gave her no leeway. There's got to be leeway in gardening.

Of course, there is another thing you can plant right now which will reward you with almost immediate flowering, and that is almost any kind of chrysanthemum. For these spectacular fall flowers are extremely easy to transplant, even in full bloom, if you dig up the roots well-encased in a good ball of earth, and give them a thorough soaking after they are set out. Chrysanthemums are so prolific that if there is a grower in your neighborhood you should be able in August or early Sep-

tember to get heavily budded plants without any difficulty. Or you may have some in a reserve bed which were divided in spring.

But chrysanthemums have an air of coming in when they should, like any conventional flower. Which is why, in August, when a person longs for something unexpected, the gardener finds a special kind of excitement in colchicums and autumn crocus. Be careful, however, when you plant them. They may suddenly bloom right in your hand.

Bulbs easy to get and to grow

When the Germans crunched across the Netherlands that spring the gardener walked down the path between two double columns of pink and white tulips, and wept. Not because these might be the last tulips she'd ever get from Holland, but because of all the garden these wede the flowers that spelled out the low country in her mind. This had been their first spring in America. They were tall and fine, and looked up at a peaceful sky.

And now for a while there won't be nearly so many tulip bulbs for sale; there will be hardly any hyacinths at all. But the gardener will get along; in fact, she's already found out through this misfortune that as far as spring-flowering bulbs are concerned, there have been all along in this country many mines of rather neglected material. As a matter of fact, if we aren't going to get tulips from Holland, it won't be long before they'll be grown right here in great enough quantities to supply the regular demand; just as we now raise an enormous number of narcissus.

In the meanwhile, she's going in for some of the things that up to now she's been skipping in the catalogues. Calochortus, for instance—called mariposa (or butterfly) tulip, though not, of course, botanically a tulip. They're less expensive, and more exciting, when bought in mixed colors and varieties, for they range from white through lavenders, pinks, purples and reds, with many different and delicate butterfly markings toward the center of their two to four inch tulip-like flowers that flare up from the tips of their one to two foot branching stems. She's planting them in clusters of ten, in patches of sandy, gritty loam, four inches deep.

Then, to take the place of grape hyacinth for the time being, she's planting a patch of triteleia under the fringes of the forsythia. This little spring-flowering bulb produces a low-spreading carpet of blue in the spring, about three inches high; and wherever I've seen it growing, I've been told enthusiastic tales of its hardiness and its quickness to cover the ground.

Another very hardy native bulb that the gardener is now getting ready to plant for the first time is camassia. The variety she's chosen for this fall is *Camassia leichtlini*, which grows from two to three feet high and comes in various shades of blue, as well as in creamy white, blooming for quite a spell in the spring in spikes of large starry flowers. It's one bulb that flourishes in almost any kind of soil, from soggy to sandy, and in sun or semi-shade.

Brodiaea she's had in the garden for some time, at least the variety coccinea, called Floral Firecracker—and well named, for its eighteen-inch stems in May are capped with crackling crimson flowers. But now she is trying a much smaller relative—Brodiaea splendens, with clusters of golden yellow (which is why they call it Golden Star) on six to eight inch stems. They aren't too particular, but the gardener is putting them where it's rather gritty, setting the bulbs three inches deep, and waiting for another part of next spring's surprises.

Four new kinds of bulbs are all she cares to manage in a single season, though there are many more native-born types that she could try, and eventually will, no doubt. She's been busy with a bargain box of undersized narcissus bulbs, setting them seven inches deep under the apple tree, where they will flourish indefinitely. And I notice that in her basket she's got the tulip bulbs she dug up last summer to keep them safe for this emergency, and is planting them again in the border for another spring under peaceful skies.

A fall collection of bulbs

Every September for the past few years the gardener and I have sat down with the bulb catalogues, and every December we have looked up from our frenzy to find that the ground was frozen and occasionally covered with snow. And consequently every spring, when the places were bare that might have been blooming, there would be something in the gardener's glance which made me feel that this was all my fault. I will admit that I may have been hypnotized by the pictures and by the descriptions that glowed in words of four colors, and thus at great length have written out too large a list; but it was really the gardener herself who could never quite make up her mind how to prune my selection to a size we could afford. At any rate, by the time our list was ready to send, we would have had to dig our holes with dynamite. And of course it was much too soon for the following fall.

So this year the gardener took the first catalogue that came, turned at once to the page of collections, and without any hesitation sent an order in for Offer No. 21. This was called a Small Garden Assortment of Spring-Flowering Bulbs for Continuous Bloom From March to June, and it contained twenty-five each of snowdrops, chionodoxas, crocuses, scilla sibiricas, grape hyacinths, bedding hyacinths, narcissuses, single early tulips, cottage tulips and Darwin tulips.

We had never bought a "collection" of anything before. Even her little packets of annual seeds the gardener had always picked and chosen with much inward debate as to type and variety. So when she sent for Offer No. 21, in which the choice of varieties was left entirely to the dealer, I said to myself it's like sending to the library for a novel, a biography and a volume of poems, without knowing what novel, or whose biography of whom, or which poet you're going to get. But I didn't actually say anything, because I knew the answer would be that at least this fall, finally, we would be able to plant some bulbs. And we'd know whether it was going to be Dreiser or Dickens when we opened the package.

Of course, with snowdrops it wouldn't make much difference. They would

have to be white, and the chances were they would be the single ones. As a matter of fact, they turned out to be the Giant Single, which is what I would have chosen myself. The chionodoxas, which some people prefer to call glory-of-the-snow, and which are about the size of the snowdrop, except that the flower has a more open and uplifted face, came in the sardensis variety, which is deep blue—the earliest of all the deep blue flowers, coming in March along with the crocus.

The gardener has a weakness for what she calls "cute" flowers—for Johnny-jump-ups and dwarf forget-me-nots and English daisies (and of course for pansies too); in fact, she has a little bed of all these particular pets where you step onto the porch from the lawn. And included in her category of cuteness is the crocus; though why the crocus and not the snowdrop, fritillary and squill, I can't make very clear. She says there's a difference between daintiness and cuteness, so I shall let it go at that and get on to the surprise package.

The crocuses were a mixture of colors: lavender, pale blue, purple, white and yellow, but we won't know which are which until March. It won't matter, because all twenty-five are scattered under the lilac bush back of the "cute" bed, where they won't be disturbed for quite a few years. The same procedure was followed with the squills and the grape hyacinths. The former are the blue and the white scilla sibirica, which grow to three or four inches and have drooping bell-like flowers in April; and the latter are the Muscari Heavenly Blue, if you want the book name to distinguish them from the smaller grape hyacinths; Muscari botryoides caeruieum, the blue; and Muscari botryoides album, the white. Grape Hyacinth Heavenly Blue is all you really need to know, just as all you really need to know about such a silly name as Myosotis palustris semperflorens is that it is plain forget-me-not. But I shall go into this matter of names some other time; it is a thing I take very much to heart, and I am glad the gardener is not one to spout botanical titles unless the common name is absolutely crazy.

I could have done without grape hyacinths, which to my notion are rather stiff and queer, though a lot of people like them; and the gardener confessed that she would have asked for something else if they hadn't been part of the collection. Even so, I'm sure the dealer would have given her twenty-five more crocuses instead if she'd only said how much she liked them. Anyhow, we put the grape hyacinths in the grass at the far end of the lawn, where a yellow foam of forsythia will break over them in April. The Heavenly Blue variety is about fifteen inches high, very bright and fragrant, and of course it is possible we may grow fonder of it as time goes on—which is often true of things you plant under protest.

The scilla sibirica, or Siberian squill —in this case I think I like the Latin name a little better—are quite small and delicate-looking, though goodness knows, hardy enough, and we have naturalized them in patches close against the shrubbery on the side of the lawn. We have done the same with the snowdrops and the chionodoxas—which Latin name, with its accent on the "ox," we prefer to the common name, as the gardener never knows whether to call them glories-of-the-snow or glory-

of-the-snows, and in either case it is too pretentious for such a simple flower.

It has become rather popular to plant all these small, early, spring-flowering bulbs right in the lawn, and I have seen several lawns not merely sprinkled with them but actually drenched. I like this effect in long grass, such an effect as daisies make in a meadow, but I want my lawn to be a neat and even green, with no flowers—not even a dandelion. A lawn is essentially an artificial fancy, close-cropped and clean, like a carpet; and even though most of these little bulbs bloom very early, they aren't always early enough to be out of the way before the rolling or the first mowing. And besides, I like the little flowers better as a ground garnish against a bank of shrubbery. Around the base of a tree on the lawn is not so bad, but all through the grass, like confetti on a carpet, seems to me to be carrying the word "naturalization" a little bit too far.

We couldn't make up our minds where outside to put the bedding hyacinths, so the gardener decided to keep the bulbs indoors in a cool dark place, and then, later on, to begin planting them, at intervals of a few weeks, in bowls, in a special kind of prepared bulb fiber containing plenty of plant food, and letting them bloom for us all winter in the house.

The twenty-five narcissus were all different. It turned out that the gardener had made this one request when she sent in her order, simply to satisfy her curiosity about this beautiful and entertaining family of flowers. The dealer didn't identify each bulb, but he did enclose a list of the twenty-five varieties, so there was nothing to do but

[Continued on page 79]

Perennials on Parade

A border like this is one of the greatest rewards a gardener can get for his patience with plants. I know there is a lot to be said for the satisfaction of raising fine individual flowers, but a succession of bloom, extending from spring to fall and recurring year after year, is a matter of lasting excitement. It is all the pleasures of gardening rolled into one.

This border is composed entirely of perennials—that is to say, of plants which customarily keep on coming up year after year. We wanted this to be succession of bloom in every sense of the words, so we eliminated the annuals, which, as a rule, come up from seed, flower and die, all in a single season. Here we have comparative permanence.

The full thirty-six-foot length of the border is shown running across the top of these two pages, and the same full border is shown below. The extraordinary contrast that has taken place between the two is nothing whatever but Nature. We emphasized the seasonal changes by planting the border so that one half of it would always be at the top of its form. In other words, when the left-hand half of the border, in the late-spring period, labeled May-June was at its peak of perfection, the right-hand half was attractively gathering itself for the splendor that came to a climax a month later when it, in turn, was photographed for the picture labeled June-July. At which time the glory of the left-hand half was receding and giving way to the advancing beauties of midsummer bloom which reached their height for the photograph labeled July-Aug. In the meantime the right-hand half was gradually changing from its early-summer aspect and building up for the brilliance of fall, when it was photographed with the designation Aug.-Sept.

In each of the four periods you will notice one special type of plant predominates. In the late-spring aspect it was the various irises.

May-June

July-Aug

June-July

Sept.-Oct.

In the early-summer period it was the delphiniums. In midsummer it was the phlox, and in the fall it was the several kinds of asters. This scheme of planting is one which anybody who hopes to achieve a rich succession of bloom would do well to follow.

Once these principal plants were planted, the iris masses intermingled with the phlox, the delphinium with the asters—all, of course, with regard to height and color—then the other plants, as indicated here by the pictures and captions, were located for the parts they were to play as accompaniment to the principal theme.

This border was made to serve as a suggestion and inspiration, not as the final answer to succession of bloom. The answer to that would be your willingness to learn the habits of the various perennials, your perseverance and your pains.

Act. 1. The border at the top of the next page is at the height of its late-spring splendor. The tall clump at the left in back is white Siberian iris; the one at the right, a purple variety. The middle rows begin at the left with lemon day-lilies, continue with coralbells and a purple mass of speedwell. The tall bearded iris run in various colors, from yellow, back of the speedwell, to russet, at the right, where they meet the daylilies and lupines. Hardy pinks make a low, scattered edging.

Act 2. This half of the border [June-July] was planted with some perennials which would be at their best in early summer and some which would bloom in the fall, as can be seen by comparing this picture with the one below. The height here is furnished by hybrid delphiniums in purples and blues, and by the tall yellow flowers of meadow-rue. The white lilies are Regals, the orange ones are Lillum croceum. The medium masses of intense blue are the delphiniums bella donna and chinense.

Act. 3. Here in midsummer heat is the small half of the border shown above in the freshness of late spring. Notice that the iris foliage is still in evidence and still effective. Hardy garden phlox is of course the main event, with salmon, pinks, red and white along the back and middle. In the center are Shasta daisies. The purple blue at right is spike speedwell; in front is dwarf balloonflower. Burning bright in the right corner are tiger lilies.

Act. 4. You can recognize this as the same right-hand half of the border shown above from the delphiniums which, having been cut back before going to seed from the June blooming, are having a second blooming here in the fall picture. The hardy asters, which predominate in this picture, were only low clumps of foliage in the June-July period, and they range from deep Red Rover on the left to white Mt. Everest on the right. The pink crysanthemum in the left center is the famous Amelia.

A planting plan for Perennials on Parade

The numbers on the planting plan refer to the first, or key numbers on the planting list beside it.

Each square on the plan represents one square foot.

The number of plants indicated in a space of certain size on the plan will approximately determine the distance apart.

We have purposely refrained from naming the "named" varieties in each case of such things as phlox, iris and asters, as any one of several varieties will answer the same purpose.

Items which can be raised with comparative ease from seed sown during the spring and summer are marked with one asterisk.

The fence is four feet high; the edging seven inches. The fence and edging are made of wooden strips, seven eighths of an inch thick and two and seven eighths wide, spaced one and a half inches apart, and painted white. The posts are natural color so as not to break the horizontal effect.

The border should have full sun for at least a good part of the day, and should be protected from severe winds.

The preparation of the bed, the fertilization and treatment of the soil, and the care of the plants, are matters which are fully discussed in any good garden guide, as well as in various pamphlets on many gardening topics issued by the Ladies' Home Journal Garden Information Service.

It must be reiterated that the border as pictured and described in the article is offered as a *suggestion* and *inspiration* rather than as a *formula*. Perennial gardening is a matter of trial and error, success and failure, and constant experimenting. You may not be able to achieve a border like this in one year, or even in two, but if you have patience and a passion for gardening, you won't mind waiting.

1.—Iris sibirica, tall white variety
2.—Iris germanica, tall yellow variety
3.—Iris germanica, tall purple variety
4.—Iris sibirica, blue medium tall variety
5.—Iris germanica, mauve medium tall variety
6.—Iris sibirica, tall blue (Perry's) variety
7.—Iris germanica, mahogany medium variety
9.—Phlox tall pink variety
10.—Dianthus plumarius pink variety* } inter-
   —Platycodon dwarf blue* } mixed
   —Nepeta mussini
11.—Phlox paniculata, tall white
12.—Phlox paniculata, tall red
13.—Phlox paniculata, medium pink
14.—Hemerocallis early yellow low
17.—Lupinus polyphyllus luteus*
18.—Phlox paniculata, tall white
19.—Lilium tigrinum
20.—Heuchera Sanguinea (Rosamunde)
21.—Shasta Daisy Alaska
22.—Phlox paniculata, salmon medium
23.—Phlox paniculata, pink, dark-eye, low
25.—Statice latifolia
26.—Artemisia Silver King*
28.—Veronica longifolia subsessillis*
29.—Veronica amethystina*
30.—Veronica amethystina*
31.—Thalictrum glaucum*
32.—Thalictrum glaucum*
33.—Lilium regale
34.—Lilium regale
36.—Plumbago larpentae* } interplanted
   —Linum flavum* }
37.—Plumbago larpentae } interplanted
   —Linum flavum }
38.—Chrysanthemum Amelia
39.—Dwarf Aster red
40.—Dwarf Aster pink
41.—Dwarf Aster white
43.—Statice latifolia*
44.—Shasta Daisy*
45.—Statice latifolia*
46.—Lilium Croceum
47.—Lilium Croceum
48.—Lilium Croceum
49.—Hardy Aster red medium
50.—Hardy Aster pink medium
51.—Hardy Aster tall white (Mt. Everest)
55.—Helenium autumnale superbum*
56.—Hardy Aster tall lavender
57.—Delphinium bella donna*
58.—Hardy Aster tall white (Mt. Everest)
59.—Hybrid Delphinium, ruddy purple with white
   eye
60.—Hybrid Delphinium, blue*
61.—Hybrid Delphinium, purple*
62.—Delphinium chinense*
63.—Hybrid Delphinium deep blue*
64.—Hybrid Delphinium deep blue*

plant them all in a sizable cluster on the southside of the big apple tree in back of the house, where they can grow and bloom and multiply, if they wish, as long as we live. Next April we shall try to tell the individual flowers from their descriptions in the catalogue. All these narcissuses and jonquils and daffodils are members of the horticultural family of Narcissus, though most of them in the mass are commonly called daffodils, even by the experts. I am hoping they will get along nicely together, and look well, if a little mixed, under the apple blossoms.

Finally we took out the tulips. We had put off looking at the list of varieties, because here we really had certain favorites, in addition to feeling more deeply about tulips than any of the other spring-flowering bulbs. We already had two varieties of Darwins in the hardy border, the pink Clara Butt and the pure white Zwanenburg, but these had been so beautiful in May that I don't think either one of us would have been disappointed if the dealer had duplicated them. The Darwins he sent, however, were the rose-colored Kathleen Parlow—said to be the tallest of all tulips—the purple Ravenswing, the deep red President Taft, and four bulbs of the black La Tulipe Noire. The early singles were all of one kind—the red and yellow Keizerskroon—while the cottage class, to the gardener's delight, was the pink-tipped white Picotee—the one tulip she considers cute.

We shall wait until the middle of November to plant the tulips, because the narrow bed below the wall is still full of bachelor buttons. Then we shall arrange them in rows, the bulbs five inches apart each way, and each kind

and variety together. We set all the bulbs of a particular grouping in their proper position, on top of the ground, before actually planting them. The gardener has already equipped herself with a bulb planter, which is like a large apple corer. You plunge it into the ground to the proper depth, and when you lift it up the soil comes with it, leaving a nice clean hole for the bulb. Then when the bulb is set at the bottom of the hole you shake the soil back in over it. I shall use the trowel, at least until the gardener decides to ask me to trade it to her for the bulb planter. She always thinks the tool I'm using is easier.

After we have set them all out on the surface we shall plant the tulips six inches deep to the bottom of the bulb. The snowdrops we planted about two inches, and were careful not to cover them with more than one inch of soil, so as to make certain they would flower. The chionodoxas went down three to four inches; the crosuses, three; the narcissuses, three to four, likewise the scillas; while the grape hyacinths we planted as deep as we shall the tulips. We didn't make these measurements with a micrometer, and would advise anyone not to be too meticulous. It took me a long time to persuade the gardener not to be so careful, and now she gets a lot more done and really enjoys her work.

But if you like to be careful in connection with your bulbs, you can dig the holes for all of them an inch deeper and put an inch of sand in the bottom. This is supposed to prevent rotting if the soil is inclined to be damp. And as mice and moles consider tulip bulbs a great delicacy, it is said to be a good plan to sprinkle the bulbs with naphthalene. And if you feel the need of using fertilizer, mix it in the soil underneath the bulb; not above it.

The gardener took all these precautions with the bulbs she planted—sand, naphthalene on the tulip bulbs, and fertilizer beneath the bulbs. I planted all mine plain. Not to be stubborn, but partly for the fun of gambling, and partly because I'd like to see just how much difference these things make. It certainly couldn't be taking more of a chance than the gardener took when she sent for Offer No. 21; and that turned out fine.

Late and white

The garden is darker every day now in November, but I can still see the curve of white petunias, like footlights in front; and the little crowd of white arctic daisies in the corner; and in the middle, like a group of dancers in dotted Swiss, a patch of the gardener's white roses she planted last fall.

Of course a lot of white is a fine idea, but I hadn't realized what a good idea it was until the garden began getting dark so early in the evening. Nor had I realized how welcome white could be as the garden season drew to its close. It not only stands out in the dusk, but in the daylight, too, it brightens up all those autumn flowers that, despite their own peculiar brightness, are somewhat absorbed by the surrounding highly colored foliage of fall.

As you probably know, white petunias present no problem at all. It is the one annual that the gardener never fails to raise in quantity every spring. And if she doesn't feel like starting them from seed, she buys a flatful from a local

grower, or as many small potted plants as she can afford from the florist. They go with almost any flower in the garden; and no matter how many you plant, you always wish you'd planted more—in case this occurs some spring.

As far as arctic daisies are concerned (called Chrysanthemum arcticum in the catalogues), this white fall flower is one of the hardiest perennials in its class. They begin blooming in September, and we've had them still blooming in the garden after frost. You get them from a nursery in the spring; then every spring, or every other spring, you divide the clump, plant some of the root divisions yourself, and give the rest away.

But the most amazing things right now are the roses—not only the whites, but the reds and pinks as well. It looks as though they might live up to their reputation in the song and outlast everything else in the garden, though the ones I have in mind are a new development in the rose world—the floribundas, or hybrid polyanthas.

We planted them late last November as dormant two-year olds. The dark reds, Belvedere, Anne Poulsen and Donald Prior, we set in two small panel beds beside the path, which we then filled up with white petunias this spring; and I must say they made flattering companions for one another, both ways. Two plants each of the double pink Smiles and the single pink Betty Prior were planted in a side pocket of the shrubbery border, with some Lady Cliveden delphiniums; and four plants of the double white Summer Snow in a cove of the same border across the middle of the lawn—it being this patch of white which stands out so vividly now after the sun goes down.

They blend in beautifully in every way with their neighboring plants, showing that they are a four-way flower to be used with annuals, perennials, shrubs, or with hybrid teas in a regular rose garden.

I spaded the ground deep for them a month or so before planting, working in a full pint of bone meal per plant; and as it was almost winter when they went in, the gardener immediately hilled up eight inches around each bush with soil and wrapped them in straw, an operation she plans to repeat, if necessary, at the end of every season, leveling it out in the spring and giving them more bone meal. The straw protection is not an essential, but it does no harm; and if a person has time for coddling, there is no telling when it may prevent winter damage.

Even though they've been blooming steadily now since June, with nothing but plenty of water and a regular rose spray, they're still going strong.

Goodbye to summer

Early fall, like the sound of a train whistle, affects the gardener and me in totally different ways. It makes her kind of sad, whereas I find it rather comforting. The sudden clamor of chrysanthemums is for her a fiesta of the finish, a gallant show with melancholy implications; while for me it is a signal to relax and give the garden reins over at last to Nature. A certain amount of planting still, some cleaning up, and I can look forward to spring. But the gardener hates to say good-by, even au revoir.

Not that it is anywhere near time for farewell. The garden is still quite sum-mery in spots. For instance, the delphiniums the gardener lopped off close to the ground on the Fourth of July, just before they went to seed, are blooming again, blue as the sky; not so tall as before, but bushier. And the new fall-blooming irises (which also bloomed in May) are now, with the delphinium and phlox, giving the garden an air of false expectancy.

The lupines, foxgloves and columbines she planted in her cold frame three months ago are now ready to lift and place in the border where they belong—nice flourishing little clumps, the first she ever raised from seed. The foxgloves go in the corner where the delphiniums used to be before the lilacs gave the situation too much afternoon shade; the others get full exposure. All three seemed to come very well from seed, the lupine and columbine especially.

Thanks to some rather extravagant plantings of bulbs in the last several Septembers, the place was alive this spring with daffodils, tulips, narcissuses, grape hyacinths, crocuses and snowdrops; but the gardener has either forgotten or doesn't trust her memory, for she is at it again. This time, however, in a much more moderate way. With two dozen bulbs each of the cottage tulip Picotee, the Lad tulip (clusiana) and the Water Lily tulip (kaufmanniana), she is making little mixed clumps of the three varieties in various odd corners of the lawn and garden. The clusiana and the kaufmanniana are species tulips; small, red and white, and early.

I feel she is doing the very best she can to keep her mind, now face to face with fall, on what is going to happen next April and May.

Some last minute planting

The smallest beds of all are those the gardener is still making in odd corners for the bulbs she brings home every now and then from neighborhood visits and shopping excursions. For instance, three bulbs of a new Spanish iris called Golden Wonder have been planted in front of the large bridal-wreath bush, where their great fringed yellow flowers will unfold next May against that beautiful snowbank. A half dozen bulbs of the white English iris Mont Blanc, which she couldn't resist getting at the seed store, have been put against the forsythia hedge, where, a little earlier in the spring, they will produce the foregoing effect in reverse. While other appropriate spots contain tiny clusters of guinea-hen flowers (an April item of spotted bell-like blooms known in the catalogues as Fritillaria meleagris), a few single white hyacinths (in the four corners where the garden paths intersect), and finally the smallest bed of all, containing a single bulb of Mrs. R. O. Backhouse, the pink daffodil, which was a piece of pure extravagance, as anyone will learn who prices one.

These beds of hers are so petite that she can go to town on their preparation. She digs them out with her trowel, several inches deeper than they need to be for the bulbs, and puts a layer of sand in the bottom. On this sand she then sets the bulbs and carefully fills the hole to the top with finely sifted soil mixed with a little leaf mold, sand and bone meal, pressing the whole thing down at the end and watering it well.

Meanwhile I am making a rather modest bed for the dozen single roses that should arrive now at almost any moment. These are to be two each of Cecil, Dainty Bess, Karen Poulsen, Innocence, Irish Fireflame and K. of K., but the bed, as I am making it, would handle just as many of any other not too robust-growing hybrid teas or polyanthas. It is two and a half feet wide and seven feet long—only that, but plenty for two rows of six, planted fourteen inches apart.

I have taken off the topsoil and piled it to one side, and have dug out the subsoil to a total depth of eighteen inches and wheeled it away. The bottom of the bed I have then loosened up with the fork to facilitate drainage. The good topsoil that I piled to one side I shall now mix with a wheelbarrowful of well-rotted cow manure and throw the mixture, as a permanent guaranty, in the bottom of the empty bed, covering it with a foot of good garden loam, borrowed from behind the grape arbor, which will bring the surface of the bed several inches above the ground level. In three weeks this bed will have settled and my roses will be here, ready to plant. And next spring, when I take off the winter protection of soil banked up around each plant, and the mulch of salt hay, I shall work plenty of bone meal in about the roses and border the bed with the pansy plants the gardener is now getting ready to cover.

We are not going to litter the place with leaves the way we did last winter. In fact, we are going to let almost everything shift for itself, and put frost protection only where really needed—over the roses, Spanish iris, the pansy plants we raised from August seedling. We are going to try either salt hay or straw.

[Continued on page 90]

Bed of Roses

This garden was made to illustrate here that roses like a certain amount of dressing up, that they prefer their own company, and that they are most effective when planted close together. In my opinion, white-painted wood and brick are their favorite foils, but this is a matter of taste and expediency. The main thing is to give rose beds and rose gardens a form so neatly and brightly defined that even when the roses are not at their best, the bed or garden will be a decoration by itself. This can be done with the simplest kinds of edgings and backgrounds. Then, for the sake of appearance as well as practicality, keep the bed or garden to nothing but roses, principally the hardy, everblooming hybrid teas, and plant them from twelve to fourteen inches apart. All this promotes rose health by facilitating feeding, spraying and winter protection. Roses like a deeply dug, well-drained clay loam, with well-rotted manure and bone meal worked into it. They also like a special rose spray twice a month from May to frost; but they have been known to flourish without too much coddling. Prepare the beds now, and order two-year field-budded stock for late-fall planting when dormant (or potted plants for planting any time). But look out for too cheap plants and for plants that have been used for greenhouse forcing.

Rose colors rarely clash, so enjoy mixed plantings of many good reliables like Red Radiance and the pink Radiance; orange-scarlet Margaret McGredy; yellow Mrs. E. P. Thom; white Snowbird; Paul's Scarlet Climber; and pink polyantha Chatillon for low bedding.

When a plant grows like a graceful shrub, puts on a show like a peony, then flowers on from June to frost with the persistence of a petunia, but with blossoms like a hybrid tea, it is a plant to warrant any gardener's consideration. Some catalogues call it the cluster rose, some the hybrid polyantha, but the designation floribunda is gaining ground. You can use this four-way plant among the shrubs, toward the front; you can place it here and there in the perennial border; it will take the place of an all-summer bed of annuals, or you can treat it as you would any other garden rose as a subject for the rose garden exclusively. It has hardiness, and a habit of growth which makes annual pruning not only unnecessary but almost inadvisable. As a consequence it grows on, improving its shape, from year to year. And here are some varieties I've found especially satisfactory—Summer Snow, a double white that's fine for a bright garnish against the shrub border, and blooming, for me, in the snow, literally. Smiles, a soft pink double. World's Fair, a deep scarlet semi-double. Holstein, a single, clustered red. And, of course, the beautiful Betty Prior in the picture. The delphinium is a belladonna type, called Cliveden Beauty.

Wire Garden

I should be the last one to minimize in any way the pleasures of garden making. But, with something up my sleeve, I am encouraged to come right out and say that a garden that is really a garden is ordinarily the work of years. There is first the painstaking planning. Then the long-drawn-out development. Finally a garden which may or may not be altogether in line with the original conception.

I know, of course, that many gardeners are able to take all doubts, delays and disappointments in their stride, as part of an absorbing enterprise. I know that a few can afford expert advice and the cost of creating an "immediate" effect. But for many others, who want a real garden at once, with all the fixings, a scheme that would give them this—with the waiting, the uncertainty, and much of the work and expense eliminated—would be a blessing.

Such a blessing, then, should be the garden illustrated here. For this, the first, we believe, ready-made garden ever produced, can be realized, from scratch, in less than a day. The plants will have to grow and come into bloom. But if they have been well started, either at home or in the nursery, this need be a matter of no more than a few weeks. And of course the really impatient gardener can transplant many of them in flower. However, the horticultural side can be put aside for a moment while I describe the garden itself.

The principal part of this garden is the framework of wide and heavy steel mesh on a steel frame, which, painted a weatherproof white, gives the garden its special form and character. This framework is a complete prefabricated unit of canopied arbor and garden enclosure, which comes in sections easy to assemble and fasten together. In fact, two able-bodied people, with a pair of pliers and a stepladder, should have no difficulty erecting the framework and putting on the canopy in a couple of hours. And while it will then stand indefinitely, it has this unique advantage over almost any garden, that it can be taken down and moved at will, solving the problem of the rented place and the temporary location.

This first major garden idea in many years also solves another problem—the one of the limited budget. For its most essential feature—the unit of canopied arbor and garden enclosure—can be purchased for less than a hundred dollars. The pool, which also comes ready to install, can be had for about five dollars. The cost of the paving is in proportion to that of the rest of the garden, varying slightly with your locality and the material you use. The flowers in the planting scheme illustrated here should cost no more than a few dollars, whether they are bought as seeds or as plants already started. For one of our principal objectives, after beauty and utility were achieved, was a garden within everyone's reach.

Two features which the photographs do not disclose, but which will add greatly to the garden's beauty, practicality and entertainment, are the fountain and the underground sprinkling system and the night illumination. Both the valve for the first two, and the switch for the lighting, are located in the arbor.

The wire garden has been designed to grace almost any conceivable situation, from a city back yard to a country estate. It can be set either right against the house, as above, where the arbor will act as porch or covered terrace, or it can be set apart, as indicated in the color photograph. In either case, when it is finished—as it should be on the same day it is begun—it will provide you, as every proper garden should, with an open place for the active pleasures of gardening, as well as shelter for the contemplation of your handiwork in comfort.

For the purpose of the photographs, nothing but the easiest annuals were used—except, of course, the water lily. The arbor is covered with two of the most beautiful of all quick-growing vines: cardinal climber and Heavenly Blue moonflower; while the garden itself is planted, in the corners, with two tall-growing varieties of marigolds —one the Yellow Supreme and the other the new sensational Collarette Crown of Gold. On the back on both sides is planted salvia Blue Bedder, with royal purple Improved Crego aster against the fence in the immediate foreground of the picture. Two varieties of zinnias are used in front of the marigolds—the giant dahlia-flowered

Crimson Monarch and the Miss Wilmott. In front of the salvia are clumps of Phlox drummondii in a mixture called Gigantea art shades. The various petunias, in front of the asters and on either side of the arbor entrance, are Ramona, La France and Blue. With the celosia Flame of Fire, or cockscomb, also at the arbor entrance, are some giant-branching white asters. The edging is composed of sweet alyssum Little Gem and ageratum Blue Perfection.

Annuals need not, by any means, form the only type of planting for the agrden. For instance, by planting early and late tulip bulbs after the annuals have finished in November, a fine display would begin in April and last through May. Then the bulbs could be lifted and stored until fall, and the annuals, which had been started in flats or cold frames, either at home or in the nursery, could be set out in the garden. Another delightful treatment would be to make it into a rose garden—either hybrid teas or polyanthas, or both; for the beds are perfect for the purpose, both in size and pattern.

The process of putting up the framework of the garden is made very simple by the extensions on the bottom of each vertical rod. These are plunged into the ground and will hold each section of the framework erect, the stability of which is completed by the clips which hold the various sections together. When the framework of the arbor has been set in place and fastened, the striped awning is fitted over the top and tied to the supporting rods.

The paving should be laid as indicated to form a circular opening for the pool, which is a round sheet-metal tank, painted green inside, the edge of which fits close against the slightly overhanging lip of the paving.

One of the most effective types of furniture for the arbor is that suggested by the white metal settee, chairs and tables shown in the photograph; but any kind of porch and garden furniture that is not too heavy and cumbersome can, of course, be used instead. The delicate white lines of the set illustrated here happens to fit nicely into the white wire scheme, and something similar to this is recommended.

The design of the garden is fairly flexible, and, although it cannot be made any smaller than it is shown here, it can, by additional sections, be made wider or longer if desired.

Preparing for winter

At first there were few pains the gardener wouldn't take to protect her plants from the heal and fancied ravages of winter. The beds would be heaped high with blankets of leaves, and every young shrub or tree that was exposed to the wind would have a screen of burlap.

But now her precautions are much less elaborate. Partly because she has learned that some of them were needless, partly because she is gradually eliminating from her garden all plants too tender to endure the climate without excessive coddling, and partly because a lot of our planting by this time has become fairly well established and no longer requires special protection. And as a result, the work from right now on is greatly lessened, and the winter aspect of the place is vastly improved.

As far as any mulching of the flower beds is concerned, she waits until the ground is frozen solid. Once or twice she was overanxious and covered her borders with a heavy coating of leaves before the frost was firmly fixed. So the mice moved in and went to work in peace and comfort on the roots and bulbs beneath; the ground, in addition, was late in freezing, preventing the plants from "ripening" properly; and also growth began too early in the spring for safety.

Having learned in this way that plants which are reasonably hardy are seldom injured by low temperatures alone, but by sudden fluctuations which cause the ground to "heave," and by unseasonable warmth, it is sometimes as late as February before the gardener covers the beds. Even then she doesn't overdo it any more. She puts on just enough mulch —whether it is leaves, peat moss, salt hay or straw—to shade the beds, not smother them. She avoids any mulch that holds the moisture on, or keeps the air away from her perennials. If snow would only come at the right time and stay, it would be the ideal mulch; which reminds me that this winter she plans to experiment with a mulch that looks like snow. It is glass "fiber"—actually glass—that looks like the spun candy you see at the county fair. It keeps the cold in, and lets in light and air; and while it is more expensive than most mulches, it can be packed up in the spring and used winter after winter.

What she has learned as to the plants which simply refuse to come through our winters, no matter how wisely protected, is something other gardeners will have to learn for themselves, as plants which seem not to be hardy in one place may seem to be hardy in others. She will try any plant twice. But she has learned that certain conditions in the ground prevent certain plants from coming through; the worst ground fault being lack of proper drainage. Until she found this out, and gave the wet spot in the garden some deep underground drainage with tile pipe and stones, lillies and chrysanthemums, especially, never survived the winters there, though fifty feet away they flourished.

The gardener still goes out of her way to protect any shrub or tree that has just been planted. Unless its situation is sufficiently protective, she sees that something in the way of burlap or boughs is put in place to keep prevailing winter winds from drying it out unduly, and winter sun from burning its foliage, if evergreen. Also, for such plants, a good mulch of manure or peat moss is a sound idea.

Needless to say, the gardener never allows a heavy fall of wet snow to weigh down the branches of shrubs or evergreens, or fails to break the glaze that makes bare branches so beautiful after an ice storm. These are obvious precautions. But if a gardener's observation of his plants in winter is really keen, all precautions that are worth taking become obvious sooner or later. One of them being just when to remove these precautions in the spring. Only watching will tell.

More winter precautions

A good two-finger frost has finally delivered the coup de grace, and the gardener is tucking in her border for the winter. A few years back, when she was a mere beginner, she had the perfectly natural notion that you covered up your plants to keep out the cold; but now she knows that you cover them up (if you cover them at all) to keep the cold in. So she waits for the first hard freeze before putting on the leaves.

What most plants would appreciate during the real winter months is cold storage. It isn't the frost; it's the fluctuation that generally causes the trouble. A few warm days in February, for instance, can do more damage than a solid month of zero. For this reason the gardener gives winter a chance to get thoroghly set, then does her best to keep it right there until all false springs have passed.

She has tried most of the mulches— oat straw, salt hay, peat moss, manure and leaves; and she seems to like the last best. This is largely because leaves cost us nothing but a little effort to gather. Not all leaves are good, however. We found that out one winter when we used the silver-maple leaves we'd raked up from the lawn.

They seemed to soften too easily, mat down with moisture, and form a smothering blanket over the border, which was worse than no mulch at all. Now we drive out in the late fall to an oak woods and fill a few burlap bags with these durable leaves that don't disintegrate during the winter. A six-inch layer of oak leaves keeps the ground at an even temperature, or nearly so, and yet permits a fairly free circulation of air, which is likewise important. Of course, oat straw and salt hay do the same; but these materials we would have to buy. This year, in addition to the oak leaves, we have brought in some spruce boughs, which we are going to try on one of the beds. If all we hear is true, they may turn out to be the best protection of all.

We don't bother much about the bushes. For the most part they are able to shift for themselves. But we do have two fine plants of tree peonies, and these we would guard at any cost, just as anyone would who had bought one and watched it perform. Around each one of these we erect a cylinder of chicken netting, supported by four stakes, and this we fill to the top with oak leaves. Even after we remove the leaves in early spring we keep the two bushes covered with muslin at any sign of late frost, however slight, taking no chances with the buds that are waiting impatiently to burst into bloom. Perhaps we are overcautious, but the gardener likes to have some special things to nurse.

Another winter enemy is the mouse. It likes to get under the mulch and nibble on the roots and bulbs. It also likes to girdle the bark of certain young trees. Mulching after the ground is well frozen helps to prevent nibbling, and setting a sleeve of wire mesh around the slender trunks discourages girdling.

Actually, the terrors of winter are not so great as all these methods of protection make them seem. The gardener considers a lot of it unnecesary coddling, and threatens every fall to let it go. But some instinct of sentimental feeling makes her change her mind each year, and by the first of December, unless winter is far behind, she has made everything as snug as a ship at anchor. And I think she feels better about it that way. I'm sure the plants themselves prefer it.

Time out for tools

It took the gardener quite a while to work up a suitable respect for tools. For one thing, she would go about her gardening at first in a kind of frenzy, as though she were putting out a fire that might get beyond her if she waited to find the right instrument. And for another, she would suddenly realize it was dark, or she was late for dinner, or it was beginning to rain or snow, and there would never be any time to put things away. I remember when she would rather plant tulips with a kitchen spoon than spend five minutes looking for the trowel. And every spring the melting snows would reveal various items of her equipment which we had been wondering about all winter.

Then gradually it began to dawn on her that gardening was more fun and

less effort when it was managed with the proper implements, and that you saved both time and money by treating your tools with some consideration. I must admit I was partly responsible for her new attitude, and the way I worked it was this:

First I saw that she had her own set of tools, as much for my sake as hers. I didn't bother to get her a spade or a fork, as the heavy preparation of the soil was my job. In fact, I got her only three of the long-handled tools—a light garden hoe, a small steel rake, and a combination pull-hoe cultivator. These take care of any soil-surface work, from smoothing to weeding, which can't be done on her hands and knees, her customary garden posture. The pull-hoe cultivator has turned out to be invaluable. On one side of the working end it has three clawlike tines that can be manipulated deftly through the flower bed or along the rows, tearing out small weeds and pulverizing the surface; and on the other side it has a sharp U-shaped blade that removes deep-rooted weeds like magic.

This pull-hoe cultivator has its counterpart in the gardener's kit of small hand tools—in this case much lighter, of course, and with a short handle. For fine, close-up weeding and cultivating she says there is nothing to compare with it, though where or when she's ever had a chance to make any wide comparative tests, I don't know. This tool, then, together with a pair of trowels and a light pruning scissors, comprises the hand kit she keeps, or tries her best to keep, in her flat garden basket.

I should explain the pair of trowels. One has a narrow blade and the other a wide. One is for seedlings and small bulbs, the other for large bulbs and clumps. I should explain also that the light pruning shears were the best I could buy; strong enough to trim not too heavy branches of trees, shrubs and roses, yet close and keen enough to snip off pansies sharp and clean.

The best thing was the box. This is long enough to hold the larger tools, wide enough to hold the garden basket with its small kit, and high enough to make, when the lid is closed, a comfortable garden bench; for the box is right beside the garden, where it stands as a constant reminder to the gardener to put her tools away. It stands three inches off the ground on runners, which keeps the box dry. And in addition to her tools, the gardener keeps in it a supply of stakes, twine and labels, together with a small duster and small sprayer, with ammunition for both.

Of course, she brings all her paraphernalia inside when winter comes. And the first thing she does, which she is doing now, is to clean and oil the metal parts and paint a fresh ring around the handles of her tools. Last year it was yellow; this year it is bright red. I don't know why.

Winter color for the garden

We decided it was time to do something about the garden's cold-weather complexion. Unless the place was covered with a mask of pure white snow its winter appearance was apt to seem a little sallow and forlorn; the general effect was brown; the sparkle was gone. So the gardener said if I would take care of the main effect she would attend, as usual, to the trimmings.

As I looked over the grounds one drab day in January it was easy to see that what we needed for the main effect was color. Not so much the brave (and expensive) green of hemlock and pine, or the picturesquee and unexpected green of laurel and rhododendron; in fact, not green at all so much as a lot of warm bright reds and yellows. Evergreens would be very gallant against the snow, and cheerful in the sunlight, but we wanted something that would be flamboyant.

With two dozen inexpensive shrubs and two small shrubby trees we designed a winter dress for the place which has provided a really brilliant costume for both lawn and garden. Although the shrubs are all occasionally called dogwoods, they are not to be confused with the flowering tree that whitens the spring woodland. There were five varieties: four of them with vivid barks in various shades of red, and the other with a golden bark that burns right through the bleakest winter day.

The four red-twigged varieties were Tatarian dogwood, coral dogwood, red dogwood and red-osier dogwood; the golden variety was yellow-twigged dogwood. They are now all well-formed, graceful, bushy shrubs which should grow ultimately from six to eight feet high, but I shall keep them at moderate size by cutting back, if necessary, after they have finished blooming in June; probably improving their winter color in the process. The shrubby trees were golden-barked osiers, a variety of willow; and these, which I set on either side of the lawn, are likewise improved, both as to shape and color, by courageous cutting.

[Continued on page 100]

Garden-Go-Round

It is a good thing the shape of gardens is not governed by the squareness that goes with building in general. For after the straight lines of streets and the rectangles of rooms, it is a relief to know that one place can be round if you want to make it that way.

This garden takes advantage of an existing background of Osage orange, but any close planting of tall shrubs, like common lilacs, or small trees, like dogwoods or flowering cherries, would make an even more effective enclosure. It has for its architecture an arbor just large enough for a bench and a curving embrasure of lattice fence thirty inches high. The arbor posts are three inches square; the crosspieces of the arbor roof and the double rails and posts of the fence are two by one, and the latticework, which is woven, not nailed, is made of one-by-three-eighths white-pine strips. The lumber should cost from ten to fifteen dollars and could be put together and erected by two pairs of capable hands in less than a day. Once in place, it should receive two coats of good outside-white paint.

But before the architecture should come the beds and path. And here you begin to appreciate the simplicity of a circular garden. To a stake driven into the predetermined center of the garden you attach a string with a small, sharp stick tied onto it; the distance from the stake to the stick will be half the garden's full diameter. This garden happens to have a diameter of sixteen feet, a size we heartily recommend. So with the sharp stick eight feet from the center by the taut string, you describe the garden's outside circumference on the ground that has been leveled off. Then shortening the string three feet, you describe the inside edge of the outer bed. Shortening it two and a half feet more, you describe the outside edge of the circular center bed, and your garden is marked out on the ground; but keep the center stake and string handy in case the lines get lost in the excitement.

Prepare the beds for planting by spading and fertilizing to a depth of at least a foot, using well-rotted manure if you can possibly get it. If you are going to make your path of brick or of cypress blocks, as we have here, or of stone or gravel, you can take off a five-inch layer of sod or good soil from the path area and put it in the beds in place of an equal amount of poor ground. This will leave room for two or so inches of sand or cinders under the paving material and still bring the finished level of the path even with the beds. When the beds are ready except for the final raking, it is time to set the fence and arbor in place. The fence should be given a good soaking to make it bend easily to fit the outside circle. Only the end posts need be deeply and firmly set into the ground, as the circular shape provides its own bracing.

This garden is shown with a planting of annuals, asters and petunias predominating. These could be started in flats, or bought in flats or pots from a local grower and set out, as small plants, in early summer. In which case a feasible and effective spring and early-summer blooming could be had from tulips planted in the fall before, and annual poppies whose seed can be sown likewise in the fall. But that is merely one suggestion. For this circular garden will accept gracefully almost any type of planting you care to give it, and will bring out beauties that could come only from its essential curves.

I planted the whole bright assortment in the spring, interspersing them among the shrubbery on every side, setting two of them against the house, and running a red line of them along the lower edge of the garden.

And now where our little immediate landscape was languid and dull it is as lively and brilliant as though it had been brightly painted.

The gardener, in the meanwhile, had been investigating the possibilities for the intimate touches. She wanted winter flowers, and she found them: four different kinds; and all of them have bloomed for her between Christmas and the first of March. The first, of course, was the Christmas rose, which is not a rose at all but a curious little perennial belonging to the buttercup family, with white flowers rising from a mat of evergreen leaves. The gardener has already found it blooming several times beneath a covering of snow.

The second and third of this winter-blooming quartet are also members of the buttercup family: winter aconite and Amur adonis. Both of them have large yellow flowers, the first about eight inches tall and the other twelve or more. The latter likes a little pampering and plenty of deep rich soil; but when it blooms as pictured above, it is well worth all the nursing the gardener gives it. Whereas the little Byzantine snowdrop, the fourth of the gardener's winter flowers, requires no attention after the bulbs have once been planted.

She planted all four of them on the first of September, and put them where they would get partial shade and protection. The first three, as roots, she set in small clumps of several plants each, some on the morning-sun side of the house and some in the lee of a low wall by the garden; and except in blizzard weather she visits them every afternoon. She planted the snowdrop bulbs three inches deep and apart below the coral dogwoods at the side of the lawn. They are blooming there now, like a bed of white ashes under a bright red fire.

Note: The four varieties of red-barked dogwoods are Cornus alba, Cornus sibirica alba, Cornus sanguinea and Cornus stolonifera. The yellow-twigged osier dogwood is Cornus stolonifera flaviramea, and the golden-barked osier is Salix vitellina. The Christmas rose is Helleborus niger; the winter aconite (or New Year's Gift) is Eranthis hyemalis; the Amur adonis is Adonis amurensis, and the snowdrop is Galanthus byzantinus.

Gardening in a glass box

The day after she saw that winter was definitely on the way, the gardener came home with a Wardian case—a glass box (upside down) on a base like a roasting pan. Some people call it a terrarium, but "Wardian case" is what I prefer to call it, because of the Mr. Ward who discovered, quite by accident, that a piece of sod which he brought indoors one winter and put under a glass bowl would grow into a miniature garden. His little piece of frozen turf was moved inside so as not to disturb the chrysalis of a butterfly which he found in his backyard that drear December day long ago, and the glass bowl was merely to protect the chrysalis. But when he saw the grass becoming green, and little ferns unfolding, and other tiny plants, till then dormant in the sod, begin to grow and burst into bloom, he soon forgot the butterfly, and went in for glass gardens in a big way.

The gardener is now in the woods collecting an assortment of bloodroot, Dutchmans-breeches, violets, hepaticas, wild anemones, arbutus (if she can find any), ferns and mosses. With these, and with little sticks for logs and little stones for rocks, she is going to make a miniature woodland scene in the bottom pan of the Wardian case. When this is all planted and arranged—with a mixture of leaf mold and sand for soil—she will set the pan outside to freeze until February. Then she will bring it indoors, water it, set it on a sunny window sill, put the glass cover on, and watch the plants come to life—just as though, in midwinter, it were suddenly spring.

She is also considering the possibility of still another terrarium in which to try some tropical plants—a couple of African violets, some tender ferns, small begonias, oxalis and creeping philodendron. With this one she would dispense, of course, with the freezing process; would start it off on the window sill right away, in fact.

The secret of the Wardian case is the very moist atmosphere in the practically airtight glass garden, caused by the condensation inside when the case is surrounded by the warmth of a room. A greenhouse condition is created within the terrarium which is an extraordinary contrast to the dryness of the atmosphere in the average room—a dryness quite painful to most plants, and the reason why the gardener has never gone in very extensively for indoor gardening, until now that she has suddenly decided to try terrariums.

The size or shape of the glass container is fairly unimportant. Anything will serve the purpose, from a Mason jar to an old aquarium turned upside down. I remember one garden growing luxuriantly inside a five-gallon demijohn. And, of course, you don't have to use a makeshift; you can buy terrariums of all shapes and sizes—and prices too —at the stores; and already planted, if you want them that way, which is what I would prefer myself. For one season of the year, at least, I would like to see something come up as a total surprise.

However, there is another way these Wardian cases can be used, more essentially practical than decorative, yet rather lovely at the same time, and that is for propagating cuttings of plants that like to grow in heat and humidity. This would include begonias, passion vine, dracaenas and other tender tropical items.

Liquid gardening

Ever since the gardener saw a newsreel of tomatoes growing in tanks of treated water she has been acting rather troubled. She has been much more attentive than ever to the earth. It was as though she felt the onrush of science would soon be putting her garden soil into the discard, that people would all be growing plants in liquid and bringing them into bloom with electricity. She has always been somewhat afraid of science, anyway.

But now that she has faced the fact of this newfangled notion, and after a fashion has tried it out for herself, she is no longer uneasy about the possibility of a revolution in the garden. For while a great deal will undoubtedly be done with growing plants in liquid solution, she is fairly well satisfied, now that she has tried growing a begonia in a bottle, that nothing will ever supersede the good old ground. Not that it doesn't work. It works beautifully. It has already produced amazing results, especially when done on a large commercial scale; but it is essentially a specialized process. It can no more take first place in the pleasure-gardener's affections than engines in any form can ever take the fun out of walking, sailing or horseback-riding.

Every gardener knows, or ought to know, that there are certain elements in the soil which make plants grow. And when these elements are there in the proper proportion, and are made available to the plant by watering and cultivation, the plant develops as it should. To grow plants in liquid instead of in soil, it is merely necessary to isolate these essential elements and, in the form of chemical compounds, put them in winter. The roots do not need the dirt, as such; they just need the foods which are present in all properly prepared soil. And now that these foods, in concentrated form, can be purchased, inexpensively and in a handy package with directions, anybody who wants to see for himself, or herself, as the gardener did, can do so without any trouble.

While, ordinarily, plants grown in this so-called liquid nutrient solution are grown in large shallow tanks and are held in place with wire netting and a layer of peat moss or excelsior, a single plant can be grown indoors very readily in a Mason jar or milk bottle. The plant stem, in this case, is supported by a split cork or anything else which will allow for growth, the roots developing in the liquid below—with of course no need for watering, which is something.

The temperature of the water is important, which is why the gardener waited for winter, when she could bring up a begonia on a bottle, so to speak, indoors and at a more or less even temperature of 70° F. Outdoors, except in a very equable climate, like parts of California, the temperature of the liquid has to be kept up in cool weather (winter is out of the question) by means of electric heating cables or some other method, which makes this kind of gardening rather complicated for the casual amateur.

The gardener chose a semperfloreus begonia (a rooted cutting) for her experiment, as this plant is well adapted to the liquid-diet idea. She gave a coat of black lacquer to a milk bottle—the roots want to grow in the dark—filled the bottle nearly full with water, added a small amount of the solution (following directions with almost fear and trembling), fitted the stem of the cutting into the split cork, and set the plant in place.

Since then it grows—just as well as it would have grown in a spot of soil. Even, she has been forced to admit, a little better. Her experimental side wants it to succeed, which it undoubtedly will. But her loyalty to the smooth, brown loam outdoors under the snow is causing her, I'm afraid, to hope against hope that somehow, through no fault of hers, it will finally fail.

Some bulbs for the house

The gardener's activities outside have always interfered somewhat with getting a little winter garden ready for the house. In October and November she has always been so occupied with planting bulbs outdoors that bulbs indoors in pots and bowls and pans have simply gone by the board, much to her subsequent regret from Christmas till Easter.

The whole narcissus family, which includes daffodils and jonquils, can be grown in pebbles in bowls. So can hyacinths. But tulips can best be grown for the house in bulb pans, which are just like ordinary flowerpots, only shallower. You can get three to four tulip bulbs in a five or six inch pan, but if you want a really impressive display get a twelve-inch pan and raise a dozen tulips in it, which is what the gardener is about to do.

No bulb that is being forced should be brought into the light until it has become well rooted. Paper-whites root rapidly, and if you plant a bowl of them every ten days or so you will have them blooming all winter. Just set any of the narcissus or hyacinths in a bowl of clean white pebbles, small shells, sharp sand or fiber; fill the bowl two-thirds full with water and put it in a dark place until root action starts and foliage appears. Then bring it into the light, but not too suddenly into strong sunlight.

Tulips should be planted in a mixture of equal parts garden loam, sharp sand, leaf mold or peat moss, with a little bone meal added. This can be done in November; though early rather than late. The pans should then be plunged in the ground in the shade and covered with a few inches of sand or cinders. By the first week of February, root growths should have begun; and if it has, the pan can be brought indoors, where, if all goes well, the tulips will bloom in about a month.

From my own observation I would say that except for the trouble—if you want to call it that—of getting the bulbs started, they are simpler indoor subjects than practically any other house plants. Less bothered by insects and diseases, they produce, with much less care, an abundance of beautiful bloom.

More indoor gardening

It isn't the same as outside, but the gardener is glad to have something to keep her fingers green through the winter. Nothing, however, that can't remain reasonably happy in the house, where it sometimes gets too warm, where unadulterated daylight is necessarily limited, and where the atmosphere is generally a little drier than it should be, even for us humans. The plants she keeps inside as household pets have got to accept our conditions.

As a matter of fact, the gardener's indoor plants get rather more humidity than we do, for she makes a point of setting their clay pots in shallow metal trays, with a layer of pebbles in the bottom of the tray, and water always kept covering the pebbles. This also provides bottom watering—by far the best. Or she plunges the pots in a deeper box that is filled with damp sphagnum moss. The rapid evaporation from the tray is good for us; and by keeping the room temperature around 72° F., which most of the plants like best, we incidentally do ourselves another favor.

Except for a succession of bulbs, like lilies of the valley, paper-white narcissus, daffodils and tulips, which can be started at home or obtained from the florist already started, the gardener goes in especially for foliage plants. These, in general, seem to be less difficult, and for indoor decoration they make excellent companions for plants whose chief beauty lies in their bloom. Foliage keeps right on being effective all winter. Flowers come and go.

The all-around favorites in our house are the various ivies (Hedera), particularly the small-leaved types. They spill over the pot, the tray, or the box in a deep-green cascade. The newly developed miniature-leaved variety called Merion Beauty is the best of all, the gardener believes. It is slower-growing than the large-leaved types, but it eventually makes a heavy, rich fountain of dark and light greens with its tiny foliage. The gardener always makes the front border of one box or tray with these little ivies.

That old-fashioned variegated vine called tradescantia is another favorite, for its green-and-milky-white foliage is almost flowerlike in the sunlight of the window, and it is both free-growing and undemanding. Pothos aureaus, a vine with pale-green and yellow variegations, is also a good garnish, easy to keep happy, and very colorful in spite of the fact that it doesn't flower.

The gardener has had amazing luck with a plant called Peperomia sandersii, which has a two-inch roundish leaf, striped and colored like the outside of a watermelon. The foliage stands up in thick masses from six to ten inches high. And she is not too proud to keep small plants of screw pine (Pandanus), fiddle-leaf rubber plant, and even Aspidistra elatior, rightly called cast-iron plant; for when they are nicely fronted with the various vines I've mentioned, they can be surprisingly decorative—and

they are, of course, absolutely foolproof. Winter, she feels, is no time for plant trouble.

Speaking of paper whites

Along about the middle of December the gardener brings in a large bag of bulbs from the seed store or the five-and-ten, and before you can say Narcissus tazetta the window sills are in flower and the whole place is filled with the fragrance of May. And this goes on without interruption until her attention is called to the first signs of authentic spring outside, after which everything in the house tapers off perceptibly.

The gardener's main crops of indoor blooms come from paper-whites, the universally popular tazetta type of narcissus mentioned above, which includes the golden-yellow variety known as Soleil d'Or, and the white-and-yellow orientalis type known as the Chinese Sacred-Lily. In fact, these three related narcissus are sometimes her principal crop of indoor flowers.

Compared with all other bulbs that are used for indoor forcing, the paper-whites, the Soleil d'Ors and the so-called Chinese Sacred-Lilies are by far the quickest and easiest to grow. A shallow bowl or pan of any kind, a few handfuls of pebbles, a little water and the bulbs are all you need.

If it's a question of decoration in the room, she uses a pottery or china bowl. Glass is not so good, because it lets in too much light on the roots. But what she likes best of all are ordinary bread-pans, long, short and round; roasting pans for a large fine array of bulbs; and for something a little different, biscuit tins, with a bulb in each biscuit well. She keeps a set of these various pans, enameled white, green, black or yellow, for the sake of change, on hand all the time. (In summer she keeps them filled with coleus cuttings, which is a story in itself.)

Anyhow, you certainly need more than one receptacle if you're going to keep a succession of these bulbs in flower. The gardener, for instance, plants a new batch every two weeks from now until late February, which keeps the window sills pretty well in bloom.

On an inch or two of pebbles in the pans or bowls she sets the bulbs, pressed into the pebbles just enough to hold them steady. Then she pours in just enough water to touch the bottom of the bulbs. And this she feels is important, for deeper water is apt to cause decay. It means constant refilling to take care of the loss from evaporation, but that is part of the enterprise, like weeding and watering outside—it's got to be done.

The bulbs will be rooted in two or three weeks, and will then begin to grow. It is better for them to spend the rooting period in cool darkness, bringing them to the light as soon as they show signs of green, so they won't shoot up fast and become weak and spindly.

Nothing could be easier to plant; and this, plus the fact that the gardener has had them in bloom in less than a month from planting, explains their popularity. Not to mention that, when they come into flower, they are something to see!

A leaf you like to touch

The gardener cultivates her **jade** plants with the tender shaping caress of a sculptress. That's the feeling they inspire. Some plants are for fragrance; some are for color; but the plant the books call Crassula arborescens appeals more than any plant I know to the sense of touch.

The gardener started cuttings taken from the parent plant during its period of growth, which I'll describe in a minute. Each cutting consisted of from three to five leaves on a stem. These she stuck in a pan of damp sand kept constantly moist for about a month, by which time the cuttings had formed roots and were ready for potting. She gave them a good gritty potting mixture, one part each of sand, leaf mold and garden loam, with plenty of pebbles in the bottom of each pot to make drainage easy, which is important.

The first pots were three-inch ones, and could have been smaller, because one thing the gardener's learned about crassulas is that their roots don't want too much room—or rather, when they have too much room they get too much water. They grow about six inches a year, and about once a year they should be put in one-inch-larger pots, but repotted with considerable care. That is to say, they should be taken out of their pots without disturbing the roots, which is easy, then set in a new pot, which has been bottom-filled, and then new earth filled in around.

They are about as easy to grow as a house plant can be. The gardener's plants have never given any signs of sickness, nor have there been any bugs. She keeps hers in a bedroom which has plenty of fresh air, and in a window with sunlight all morning. They don't mind warmth, aren't bothered by coolness, but they'll begin to collapse if the atmosphere becomes close.

[*Continued on page 113*]

Victorian Garden

This garden speaks for itself. Its accent and its costume are in the manner of fifty years ago, though it was made last summer especially for this photograph. It was made to remind you of the Victorian charms that are being overlooked today: the garden fences and furniture in ornamental iron, the bedding plants that bloom right through from spring to fall.

The fences and furniture are worth looking for, in originals or reproductions; while the plants are as easy to get and to grow as they ever were. Lady's slipper, canna, begonia, geranium and ageratum—not to mention that rubber plant on a summer outing, floss flower—can recall the horse-and-carriage days, even without the fixtures. Buy small plants, if necessary, and get them in as soon as the ground is warm; keep an image of primness in mind, and remember what a good gardener your great-grandmother was.

Jungle Garden

From the Phlox drummondi in the foreground beds to the castor bean behind the fence, every plant in this garden is an annual. Which means that from seed sown in the spring you get not only all this splendor, but all this shade and privacy to boot. The tropical-looking hedge of castor bean (Ricinus zanzibarensis) is perhaps the most important feature. This grows phenomenally fast—as much as thirteen feet in a few months—but it wants to be grown in a mass, like this. The various red and yellow celosias (called "cockscomb") in the tall border—which, like the caster bean, are generally mis-planted as curiosities—are here, among the marigolds, given the play their flaming beauty deserves. In the low beds down front, petunias and annual phlox carry on this way from early summer till frost. The red-and-yellow color scheme of the garden is set off and framed in more than you might imagine by the scalloped white fence of six-inch cypress boards that can be rounded off either at the mill or at home. The lumber should cost from five to ten dollars, depending upon locality; and anyone handy with tools could round off the board ends in no time. The garden-bed edging boards are long six-inch pieces, scalloped on one side . If carpenter-built, the cost might be doubled. The two-foot recess in the fence makes a place for the six-foot, built-in garden seat that, by the time hot weather has arrived (and thanks to the rapid shelter of the castor bean from Zanzibar), is a cool shadowy spot in which to sit.

How to Beat Picasso

In the first place, begin with brave color notions. Try the potency of heavy purples, burning reds, clean whites, bright yellows and rich blues. Have courage to mix in a mass of scarlet sage with the fine clear blues of Chinese delphiniums and a drift of lemon-yellow calendulas. Heighten the effect of these primary colors with pure white annual phlox—the whitest I know. Observe, in the color composition illustrated here, with what simple means, like these, a striking effect can be achieved! Be bold! Choose annuals whose blooms predominate the plant. Notice at a nursery that sweet alyssum, as an edging, is a strip of intense white; that the little Blue Stone lobelia is a line of vivid blue; in neither case are you conscious of diffusing foliage. Don't bank on zinnias for absolutely clear colors. In fact, don't take any catalogue colors too literally. "Blue" is generally lavender or purple; "yellow" is likely to be orange; and even "white" is sometimes a faded pale pink. The most brilliant beds, as far as spectacular color pattern is concerned, are those on which the eye looks down; for most flowers face up. So try keeping your plants on the low side, from five-inch lobelias and alyssums in front to twenty-inch things in back. Buy your seeds in separate colors, the way a painter buys his paints. And don't expect to plant a work of art the first crack out of the box. But lay on with courage and imagination the colors Picasso would use if he could. You've got them right there in those little packets.

Brilliant white annual phlox, feathery white babies'-breath, purple and maroon petunias, scarlet sage and blue-purple verbenas make this bed a vibrant adventure in modern planting that anyone can experience.

Once a week, during their growing period, she wipes off their leaves with a damp cloth, and every other day or so she sprays them all over with a fine mist from an atomizer, and every day she gives them a little water. This is for their growing season only, which ordinarily lasts all but two or three months of the year, during which time they'll be putting out new little leaves and showing growth on the larger ones.

But when this growing stops, the plant is ready to rest. The gardener keeps her plants right where they are all through the resting period, and there's no difference in their decorativeness. Maybe they aren't quite as freshly green, but they're still pretty beautiful. And until they begin growth again she barely waters them—just enough every day to keep the ground from getting dry.

Crassulas can get to be too big for comfort, given time and encouragement. I've heard of them eight feet tall and six feet in diameter, which is much more than the gardener has in mind. Her ambition is to get a plant not so enormous as shapely; a shapeliness that she controls by careful pruning.

Up to now we've thought of our jade plants in terms of form and foliage, but the large ones are almost old enough to flower, which, when they do, will be quite a sight—a mass of little white blossoms emerging from the leaves in early spring as a kind of extra dividend.

Cultivating the catalogues

There is a vast and fascinating field of garden literature from which fresh editions every year are sent out free of charge to anyone who can make good use of them. And although I am sure the gardener has never read a regular garden book in her life, she is now immersed in the reading matter I mention.

As you must know, I mean, of course, the seed and plant catalogues. But I also have in mind the catalogues of other types of garden paraphernalia, from tools to fertilizers—most of which are included in the literature of the larger dealers.

On the horticultural side, these publications range from simple leaflets, very matter-of-fact, to elaborate brochures, illustrated in color and positively encyclopedic. The gardener happens to prefer the former, particularly those put out by specialists, in which she can study, without distraction, hundreds of varieties of a single kind of plant—like peonies, roses, irises, dahlias. These are the monographs of the catalogue library, and many of them list and describe—more or less dispassionately—more varieties of a single plant family than you will find in a full-sized volume.

As for myself, I am fonder of the general catalogues that run the gamut of a gardener's plant material, including all his equipment. Turning the pages of one of these complete catalogues, I can imagine myself, for the moment at least, not only the successful raiser of every plant I see—for their cultivation sounds so simple and easy—but the possessor of all sorts of laborsaving utensils.

In very few garden books are plants classified so convenietnly, described in so great detail, and illustrated so profusely, as they are in a good general catalogue. And coming out once a year, or even oftener, they are always up to date, with all the latest introductions prominently displayed. And when cultural directions are included you may be sure they are pretty reliable, for it is a matter of real importance to the dealer that his plant be given every possible opportunity to succeed.

The catalogue privilege is one that good gardeners don't abuse. In fact, many dealers and growers will discontinue sending out catalogues to people who show no signs of ever becoming customers. The gardener herself does comparatively little buying, but likes to keep in touch with the new lists of her favorite seed and plant people. So when she sends for a catalogue that she knows must cost considerable, she encloses a few stamps—just to ease her conscience.

There are some people, including the gardener herself, who criticize the catalogues for their fulsomeness—for what seems a certain amount of overstatement in describing the performance and appearance of novelties especially. But this I lay to justifiable enthusiasm on the part of the catalogue people. I think every new plant deserves a flattering debut, even though it may be a little excessive. Plants, after all, are not like something you turn out on a machine. No matter how comparatively poor, they are bound to be appealing to anyone who grows them.

It seems to me that seed and plant catalogues have a special quality in a world of catalogues. Goodness knows, they have a commercial aspect; but that aspect is somehow altered by the nature of the material.

Pots and pans

I have always been somewhat bothered by the gardener's lack of respect for the paraphernalia of her craft. She would just as soon bring up her seedlings in cigar boxes and set them out with a kitchen spoon. Gardening, for her, is getting things to grow regardless. Whereas I am a lover of equipment. I can postpone practically any garden task until I possess the proper instrument. And whenever I can persuade the gardener to play according to Hoyle it justifies in a way my collection of gardening tools, which I am afraid she regards as rather extensive, to say the least.

One recently acquired and fairly large item in the garden-room array which the gardener looked upon at the time as a wild extravagance is an assortment of seed pans and flowerpots—the most functional of all garden accessories, and the most professional-looking. They have been very beautiful all winter, set out on the garden workbench; and now at last they are being made useful as well.

The seed pans, which the gardener is getting ready for an early sowing of annuals, are made of clay, like the flower-pots, and have five holes in the bottom for drainage. They may be a little more expensive than the wooden flats you buy, and of course considerably more so than the flats you make at home or the cigar boxes the gardener gets I don't know where; but they last forever, have just the proper porosity to keep the soil in condition, and, as I say, they are very professional-looking, which is a great satisfaction to anyone who takes his gardening seriously.

The gardener puts a half-inch layer of pebbles in the bottom of each seed pan, then fills the pans to within a half inch of the top with a sifted mixture of garden soil and sand in equal quantities. After smoothing the surface she sprinkles on a packet of seeds as evenly as she can, waters the pan through a piece of burlap to avoid disturbing the seeds, covers it with an eight-by-ten-inch pane of glass, and sets it out of the light. The glass keeps the soil from drying out too quickly, and makes watering every third day just about right—not too much water at any one time, according to the gardener, and always through the burlap until the seeds have begun to sprout.

As soon as the sprouts have formed two leaves, the gardener, who has heretofore picked them out gently with a stick and transplanted them from cigar boxes to various crude flats that she has accumulated, will this year, as a concession to my purchase, prick them out from the seed pans and transplant them into small individual pots.

The pots are two and a quarter inches wide as well as deep. They are just large enough for a single seedling to develop to the point where it should be transplanted into the garden.

In preparing the pots for the seedlings from the seed pans, the gardener first puts a small piece of broken pot—called a crock—over the hole in the bottom for proper drainage, then fills this pot with a sifted mixture of sand, soil and leaf mold in equal parts. They are then ready to receive the seedlings.

The question of cuttings

There was a time when the gardener was inclined to look down upon things like coleus. Her feeling was that there seemed to be something vulgar and Victorian about their lively variegated leaves, whereas a delphinium, say, had some dignity and restraint. It was the way sophisticated people with a rush of Hemingway to the head would look down upon Dickens, or the way modern music lovers would have a spell of considering Mendelssohn too melodious. But everybody comes to his senses by and by, and the gardener now couldn't get along without coleus.

The matter of taste, however, is not the point. A lot of people don't care for geraniums, or begonias—or coleus, either, as far as that's concerned. But if they'd get to know them it might be different. As when the gardener walked into a greenhouse one day, and one whole propagating bench was like a brightly colored strip of carpeting, tightly tufted with little cuttings of coleus of many varieties—red, yellow, pale green, in plain and fancy figurations. Each cutting was a cluster of leaves, like a flower, on a short piece of stem that was buried in sand to form a root and become a plant. In fact, this was the point that got the gardener—the propagating part.

For a coleus cutting is one of the easiest things there are to root—let's say the easiest—and a fascinating plant to play with. You take the cuttings from the parent plants—as many cuttings as there are stem ends—stick them in sand, keep warm and damp from below, and, when they've formed little roots, pot them singly in a sandy-loam soil, in little clay or paper pots, or in tin cans if you like, and as soon as the weather is safe, plant them outside. They offer, in this way, the simplest method of learning about multiplying plants by the vegetative process. From there, like the gardener, you will probably go on to other plants.

A shallow box of sand is all you need in the way of special equipment. You wet the sand, flatten it out with a small piece of board, scratch a line in the sand with a flat sharp stick, keeping it straight with a two-inch strip like a ruler, insert a row of cuttings, firm them in with the ruler, make another scratch two inches away from the first row, and proceed as before until the box is filled. Then you cover the cuttings with a sheet of paper for a few days to shade them and retain the moisture, then remove the paper, keep the sand damp by setting the box in a tray of water once a day, and keep the box over a radiator in a sunny window until the cuttings have formed their roots.

If you haven't got plants from which to take your own cuttings, and can't get any from your neighbors, you can either get them from the local greenhouse man or find out from him where to send for them. Some growers make a specialty of coleus, and can furnish you with a great variety for very little. From such an assortment you will soon adopt your own particular favorites. Or if you'd like to develop a lot of new colors and figurations, just get a packet of seeds of some good coleus mixture and sow them in a box of sandy loam. You will see right away the difference between propagating by seed and propagating by cuttings. By the former method, coleus not only don't come true, but are somewhat unpredictable. You might get something quite amazing, which, after it has grown sufficiently to produce cuttings, you can then by the latter method reproduce faithfully.

The gardener is always rooting a few coleus cuttings; it doesn't matter when you do it, though of course the plants won't stand for frost. Whenever she comes across a variety she's never seen before, if she likes it, she tries to get a cutting or two. Probably coleus, through the interchange of cuttings, has done more to make gardening friends than any other plant. The cuttings are a decoration from the beginning. In fact, the gardener grows them all winter in pans on the window sills. She doesn't bother to pot them up, but when they get too large for their own good, she takes cuttings off them and starts them out all over again—gay little boxes of sprouting leaves, and a fine exercise in the facts of plant life.

A winter cache

I could tell the bundle I'd been seeing in the bottom of the coat closet all winter was something the gardener had wrapped up herself; but that was as far as my curiosity took me until the day when she asked me to get it out, and I waited around to see what was inside.

Well, there were four shallow seed boxes, a paper sack of nicely sifted soil, and a smaller bag of peat moss. One of the seed boxes, which the gardener won't call by their more professional name of flats—I don't know why—was filled with flowerpot fragments, called potsherds in garden books—a word I've never heard spoken.

At any rate, the gardener took this flatful of potsherds and distributed them over the bottom of each flat, or seed box, for drainage. Then over each layer of broken crockery she spread an inch or less of peat moss, which she first dampened slightly in a dishpan. This dampening is not so easy as it sounds,

[Continued on page 122]

Gardens with Pre-fabricated Enclosures

Here we have a garden of marigolds, a garden of zinnias and a garden of scarlet sage—three of the most eloquent actors in the whole company of annual plants. But before we go into the flowers, I would like to have you look at the settings we have created. For in a way the principal part in each of these gardens is played by this new and versatile type of enclosure—its first appearance in public.

Each setting is made up of a number of similar units, each unit being a v-shaped section of wooden fencing. The v shape enables each unit to stand up alone, firmly, and without any further support. The v shape also enables you to outline gardens of various designs, such as those illustrated here.

The marigold garden, for instance, is an arrangement of six v-shaped units, not all of them completely visible, forming the background, against the pines, at the end of a long walk. The zinnia

garden is an arrangement of eight units, forming an effective enclosure at the intersection of two paths; while the scarlet-sage garden is a version of the serpentine-wall idea which could be extended indefinitely to form a background for a long border.

With this new type of garden enclosure that we have devised, you can make your garden larger or smaller at will, change its shape whenever you wish, or, without any trouble, take your setting with

you when you move. It can be a permanent fixture; or it can be taken up and stored in winter as compactly as a nest of saucers.

The construction is simplicity itself. Each v-shaped unit of fencing consists of two panels fastened together with angle irons. Each panel is thirty inches high and thirty-six inches long, and is built up of a double thickness of boards six inches wide and three-quarters of an inch thick, the boards on one face of the panel being laid vertical and the boards on the other face horizontal.

The ground on which these garden enclosures are placed must be both level and solid. When the whole enclosure has been set in place and the connecting ends of each unit have been fastened together with three-inch nails, the only remaining carpentry is the fitting on of a one-by-two-inch coping strip, which can be clearly seen in the photograph of the zinnia garden.

The planting in the three gardens is somewhat incidental to the enclosures, which is why, in each case, there is featured but one type of annual. However, the simplicity of the three plantings does not diminish in any way their effectiveness. The color variety among marigolds and zinnias is sufficient to make straight plantings of them constantly beautiful from midsummer to frost, while the solid brilliance of scarlet sage, especially when interspersed with the tall and graceful spiderflower, is positively breath-taking.

The zinnia garden in the photograph is made up of eight units of the prefabricated volume. In the garden of scarlet sage and white spiderflower the enclosure is shown in an adaptation of the serpentine-wall idea.

The new type of garden enclosure is also shown as a background for marigolds, garnished with lobelia, at the end of a walk.

for while peat moss can absorb an incredible amount of water, it takes its time about it; of course, once wet, holding the moisture indefinitely, which is the whole point.

Over the peat moss layer the gardener then spread the nicely sifted soil from the paper sack, filling each flat to within a quarter inch of the top. And it was here that I heard why the bundle had been in the bottom of the coat closet all winter. I should have known that soil for seed boxes is not always easy to get in late winter, or even in very early spring. If it isn't frozen solid outside, it's soggy; and in any event, it isn't ready to use. The gardener had learned about this from experience; so last fall, with extraordinary foresight, she made up this bagful of seeding mixture. Equal parts garden loam, leaf mold and sand, thoroughly mixed and sifted. And as four small seed boxes don't require much soil, she decided to take a precaution that was very professional indeed. She put the soil mixture in the oven and baked it; thus not only destroying all the weed seeds, but, through sterilization, preventing any plant ailment that might have emanated from the raw soil.

After the gardener had smothered over the surface of the soil in the seed boxes and pressed it evenly with a block of wood, she gave each flatful of soil a good soaking with her rubber-bulb sprayer. Then she lined out rows with the edge of a plant label, planted her seeds, right from the package, but not too thickly; sprinkled just a trace of the fine dry soil over them, and pressed down lightly with the block again, and labeled everything. She then set the flats on a board above a not-too-warm radiator and cov-ered them with paper, as bottom heat, darkness and something to prevent evaporation are all good things for germination.

What did she plant? Well, one flat is all ageratum—the newish dwarf Blue Cap. Another is filled with a new verbena, called Blue Sentinel, supposed not to have the bad spreading habit of this otherwise exemplary annual. The third flat will give her an early start with a recent rosy petunia, called Hollywood Star, with pointed petals; while the fourth is filled with bedding begonias, to give the garden a Victorian touch this summer. The rest she'll plant outside as soon as the ground is right.

And somehow or other she managed to crowd in, as well, some replacements for her herb garden—notably borago and basil.

The spring awakening

The gardener makes quite a point of the fact that her field of operation is the flower bed. She says that as far as gardening is concerned, she is willing to wait for spring—though "willing" is hardly the word. For there has been one bowl of bulbs after another in bloom on the window sill ever since Christmas, all of which from crocus to tulips, will be repeated in the garden at the proper season outside. And right now the fireplace is flanked with golden boughs of forsythia that the gardener has forced into flower a full month in advance of the still bare bushes from which these branches were cut. So it would seem she isn't as willing to wait as she thinks. Beautiful as they are, the bulbs and goldenbell denote a great deal more to her than decoration. She may not realize how much they are snatches of her garden to defy the frost in the flower beds, or how much they are a poultice for her impatience.

Another late-winter solace for her is the raising of something from seed. For her seeding episode this year she has changed over from flats to bulb pans, just to try something different—besides having the bulb pans in the house. These so-called pans are nothing but shallow flowerpots, made of the same red porous clay—no glaze. She fills a six-inch—in diameter—pan with a seeding-soil mixture of one third sand, one third leaf mold and one third garden soil to within an inch of the top; having provided drainage in the bottom with first a layer of gravel and then a layer of dry leaves. Then having firmed the soil absolutely smooth with a small cake tin, she scatters the seed evenly over the surface right from the packet and covers the seed with a film of soil which she then presses gently down with the cake tin.

As the watering of seeds is a delicate operation when done directly or even when done through a cloth, the gardener this time is using the absorption method. Having sown her seeds in a six-inch pan, she sets this pan inside an eight-inch pan—one inch larger all around. An inch or more of sphagnum moss in the bottom of the larger pan, and the inch space all around the sides filled in also with the moss. By keeping the moss damp at all times, the soil in the seed pan will always be held at just the right degree of wetness without ever having to put water on the seeds.

After these preparations, the gardener places a small pane of glass over the pans to hold the humidity around the

seeds and puts a piece of paper over the glass to keep them dark until they have germinated. Frosted glass would do both. She keeps the pan in the pantry, where it is neither too warm nor too dry, until the seedlings appear, when she puts it on almost any sunny window sill and removes the glass and shade. Then when the seedlings have sprouted their second pair of leaves she lifts them out, a tablespoonful of seedlings at a time, selects the largest and thriftiest, and plants them singly in two-and-one-half-inch pots, filled with the same soil mixture.

Two dozen pots fit nicely into a twelve-by-eighteen-inch flat, and the gardener seldom pots up more than that many seedlings. The tending of twenty-four plants to set out when real gardening begins is all she needs to satisfy the itch in her fingers and give her a good green start when she finally gets to her flower beds.

The question of a cold frame

What with alternating frost and thaw, early April weather combines the worst features of both winter and spring. Gardening in the open ground is not only unpleasant; it is practically impossible. But the gardener, who would ordinarily be as frantic as Donald Duck, with everything balmy one minute and bitter the next, is apparently unconcerned. For she has finally found a way to outwit the season, though goodness knows the way has never been anyone's private affair. She has merely gone in for glass.

She began with a glass-covered box that was really meant for the clump of

Christmas roses in the garden. With this for protection she was determined to bring these plants into bloom on the day denoted by their name, as it is their custom with us to flower in January or February, if at all. But this December was so sunny and mild that our Helleborus niger, as they are known horticulturally, blossomed without the help of the box—right on the dot. She kept it instead over a couple of early tulips, and when these flowered six weeks ahead of time she became so enamored of the glass idea that she persuaded me to make her a small edition of the cold frame I was building for myself.

The one I made for her is three feet square, which is six times the size of her glass-covered forcing box, but at that only one sixth the size of the one I am making. Mine, I sometimes hope, will be too large for her to handle. The four sides of hers are made of one-inch-thick unfinished cypress, a wood that rarely ever rots. The board in back is twelve inches high, the one in front is eight. The upper edges of the two side boards are therefore cut on a slope. To make it still easier for the gardener to manage, I hinged to the back board a sash onto which I fastened a square of the glass-like cloth that is now quite often used for this purpose, and which is less heavy and, of course, much less breakable than glass. You can buy a cold frame like that, ready-made, for about five dollars. This one cost about two, not counting my time, which belongs to her anyway.

We set the finished cold frame on a perfectly level empty patch of the gardener's annual bed in the southeast angle of the house, where it gets all the warm sun and none of the cold wind— the low front side facing due south, to catch as much light as possible. This turns out to be a convenient location, because now that the gardener has set in the cold frame the two flats of seedlings she started indoors, hardening them off for planting out in the garden later on, and has even sown in it several rows of seeds, for which the open ground won't be fit for another month, she can easily reach the frame for the little attention it requires.

This is mostly keeping the sash open or closed, depending upon the weather. She keeps it open an inch or two whenever the sun it out, unless it is actually freezin. On really warm days she keeps it open wide; but having no faith in the weather at this time of the year, she is pretty watchful. At night she keeps it closed.

In the summer she plans to use her cold frame for starting her perennial seeds and for rooting her cuttings. For this purpose I shall have to make her a slat cover of lath, which will provide the necessary shade and replace temporarily the glass-cloth sash that will go back on again as soon as cold weather returns.

The gardener speaks now of a whole row of frames. Before I know it she will be talking about a greenhouse. So it's a good thing May will be here in a month.

A Garden for Good Companions

Tulips and chrysanthemums make good bedding companions; for by the time your tulips have finished blooming you can get small chrysanthemum plants in pots, grown from the division made from old plants in the very early spring. And you can then intersperse these small chrysanthemum plants among the fading tulips, locating and spacing them according to their eventual heights and spreads. As soon, then, as the tulip foliage has fully ripened, it can be cut off and removed, leaving plenty of room for the chrysanthemums to develop.

Where tulips and chrysanthemums share the same space in the garden, it is a good plan to plant the tulip bulbs deeper than ordinarily—the bottom of the bulb about nine inches down, to avoid undue disturbance from the chrysanthemum roots.

After the chrysanthemums have finished blooming, and just before heavy frost, you can lift the chrysanthemum plants and set them elsewhere in a sheltered, well-drained row, from where, in late winter, the ones you wish to increase by division can be lifted with a clump of earth and thawed out in a coldframe until it is ready for division—a very simple operation.

The choice from the catalogue list gets wider and more tantalizing every year as the hybrids multiply, but some of the older varieties are going to be hard to beat, and are usually less expensive. There are kinds like Cydonia, the terra cotta that glows in three dark patches across the middle ground of the garden; like the yellow-centered, salmon-petaled single Sensation, seen above and beneath the birdhouse; and like the flecked orange-bronze double Rapture, that stands in two tall piles against the fence. Then for pinks, pure whites and clear yellows, respectively, you have, in the foreground, the famous Amelia, the early and long blooming Clara Curtis, the immaculate Princess and the dazzling Sappho.

Annuals on Parade

You more or less have to wear a garden of perennials for a good many seasons, but you can put on a new costume of annuals every spring. Every year a chance to step out in a different horticultural dress, with so many materials from which to choose that you never need repeat yourself in general effect, even though you do keep on with a few reliable favorites. With all the fresh new seed catalogues running over, I often wonder why gardens follow the same old floral patterns, time after time.

Here, for example, in identical settings, I have suggested two possibilities from the almost inexhaustible variety of color schemes and plant effects which annuals can produce. Flanked by two large rose-of-Sharon bushes, whose midsummer bloom comes at a slack season for shrubs, the lamplit gateway is further framed in wings of wideboard fencing which are smothered with morning-glories. And it is with these two annual vines that the color difference between the two settings first appears. For in the pink-and-white scheme, the climbing background is made up of the morning-glory named Scarlett

O'Hara; while in the border of blue-and-yellow effects below, the morning-glory cape on the fence is the celebrated Heavenly Blue. In the former garden is carried out the color keynote of the Scarlett O'Haras with Rosy Morn petunias, pink and red varieties of Phlox drummondi, the new pink annual hollyhock called Indian Spring, and with Easter Greeting dwarf dahlias for their all-summer white—even though they aren't annuals, but grow from tender tubers.

Down from the Heavenly Blues in the other border are various clear-yellow marigolds, some black-eyed Susans, and the new golden, quick-flowering pansy, Sensation, with the blue choirs made of Chinese forget-me-not (known as Cynoglossum firmament) and cupflower (called Nierembergia hippomanica in the catalogues), the latter being one of the best lavender-blue edging plants in existence, living up to its reputation till frost.

It is a good idea to start the nierembergia and the cynoglossum fairly early indoors, so that they can be set out in the warm ground as either transplanted seedlings or preferably plants from small pots. As for the Heavenly Blues, I have always found the variety Clark's New Early Improved to be as good as it sounds, and I have found that potting the seedlings in four inch pots, giving each plant a four foot bamboo stake to climb on, then setting them out when they reached the top of the stake—I have found this method to give the best results. This morning glory, or Ipomaea, has always seemed to bloom better when set out in somewhat meagre soil, not spending the energy gained from excess nourishment in a great crop of leaves with few flowers. And of course to groove or soak the seeds before planting facilitates germination.

The obvious point in these two pictures is to discourage the indiscriminate mixtures which make up most beds of annuals; for it is certainly true that colors can easily be controlled—right from the catalogue on.

Succession of Bloom in a Window Garden

The kind of window gardening presented here is more than a matter of green fingers and a good florist. It is the gentle pastime of cultivating indoor plants carried to its logical conclusion: which is to make them perform an attractive feat of decoration.

Raising plants successfully and keeping them in healthy condition, are, of course, important parts of the process; but arranging them in well-ordered designs, and paying proper attention to their seasonal activities, are the things which make an entertaining art out of a pleasant but essentially practical enterprise. The requirements are fairly simple: a certain tender attitude toward plants plus a real desire to understand their problems, a feeling for form and color, and last but not least—a window. We'll have the last, at least, and the rest can be easily acquired.

This window garden begins just about the time the final chrysanthemums are fading in the borders outside and ends with the poking up of crocuses through the early spring lawn. It covers the four full months or more which, in most parts of the country, would find the gardener with nothing to do outdoors. The time it takes to care for such a window as this need not be more than a few minutes a day, but there won't be a moment from fall till spring when the garden will not repay in beauty, entertainment and interest all the care and attention you feel inclined to give it.

Due to the developing habits of the various plants, the window falls naturally into four different effects as time goes on, each one lasting in prime condition for several weeks at least, and some for quite a little longer. And as the climax of each effect happens to coincide with a holiday, there could be no better way to mark the progressive scenes of the window garden than by Thanksgiving, Christmas, St. Valentine's and Easter.

We have used a dozen different kinds of plants that can be raised from seeds, roots or cuttings if you wish, or bought ready potted from the florist; four different kinds of indoor-flowering bulbs that can easily be grown at home from the bulb to maturity; and two or three kinds of vines.

In addition to these growing plants, we have used (in the first setting) a bowl of cut nasturtiums—the last of the summer's crop, and (in the Easter scene) two bowls of forsythia, cut early and forced into flower indoors.

Some of the plants, such as the orange tree, the poinsettia, the primroses and the calla lilies, while by no means impossible for the amateur gardener to raise, are more likely to come as holiday or birthday gifts, or as a mild extravagance on the part of the household itself. All the rest are, as they say, "of very simple culture," and well worth the satisfaction you get from having brought them into maturity yourself.

For all these charming effects any sunlit window is suitable. If only a window with a northern exposure is available, then the pictures must be created with ferns and vines as the domiant notes and African violets, cyclamens, and ever-blooming begonias for the flowers. Of course, the white-margined English ivy, the cream-edged periwinkle, and the golden Ceylon creeper may be introduced for constant variation amid the definite green.

The four seasonal arrangements illustrated grow on glass shelves with adjustable fittings. These are available in any department store.

Some shade, Venetian blind or curtain is advisable near the glass. On bitter nights this is drawn to keep away the icy blasts and to prevent the plants from coming into direct contact with the cold windowpanes. Protection is also needed at times from strong sunshine, particularly during early October, when the garden is first set up, and again in late spring, when the sun is hot and so bright it fades the delicate freesias, callas and cyclamens, if allowed to beat down upon them for long, unguarded hours.

Once shelves and shade are in place, the indoor garden is ready for planting. By Thanksgiving its autumn glory is apparent, especially in the permanent green tracery which frames the window lieu of a drapery and is the first concern of the gardener. Yet the Japanese grape and the heart-shaped philodendron now give only a promise of their rampant power. In a single season they grow remarkably, and the second spring display so much *joie de vivre* that trimming is frequently necessary to keep their eagnerness in window bounds.

The florist provides these vines potted in a balanced soil mixture, but during all periods of healthy growth—never in times of inactivity or rest—they are much benefited by additional feeding. I keep a covered jar of liquid manure on hand for all my plants and apply it every three or four weeks after thorough watering of the soil. Any of the prepared cow-manure products may be used to make such an infusion. Just add the dry material to the water and let it stand for several days. Then stir it up and apply the liquid diluted to the color of weak tea. From one-quarter to a whole teacupful is enough for each plant, according to its size. Commercial plant foods or plant tablets may be substituted and used acording to the manufacturer's directions.

The reliable philodendron also thrives on a water diet in the cobalt-blue jars at the first window. A few drops of the liquid fertilizer are added weekly to keep it fit. This is conveniently done at the time extra water is supplied to make up for evaporation.

On the sill and in the Brittany kitten vases are cuttings of the new self-branching English ivy, but any of the ivies—the green, variegated or miniature English types—could be used, since all are reliable for soil and water.

Cuttings of ivy for winter, however, if taken from the outdoor garden, are best secured in late August and placed for a month or longer in a pail of water set in the shade. Then by the time the window garden is ready in late September they will be well-rooted and ready to thrive in the less agreeable atmosphere of the indoor world.

At the table's edge the Sprenger variety of asparagus fern casts interesting shadows. This plant is as undemanding as it is beautiful, and in a rather sandy soil makes actual yards of growth through the winter.

Numerous other plants suggest themselves for the perennial green. The Chinese evergreens on the second shelf make a pleasant tracery against the light. A variety of such ferns as the holly, Boston, Whitman's, and Victoria is pretty for sunless windows.

But a succession of bright colors is the sight every woman craves in the window garden, and this is much easier to obtain than the

ST. VALENTINE'S   EASTER

THANKSGIVING   CHRISTMAS

steady brilliance of these pictures suggests. To achieve constant bloom, a maximum of sunlight is essential—all that the brightest east or south window can admit. Even then, during certain long, gray winter weeks there will be too little to keep the geraniums at work and they will have to go on vacation for a time elsewhere.

At Thanksgiving, however, geraniums and wax begonias are in their prime, proving at the start that they are the two most reliable window-garden plants available. Geraniums for winter bloom are best started from May or June cuttings of older plants. Tired plants from the summer window boxes will hardly set a blossom until spring, as in addition to sunshine the geraniums require a rest. They will flower profusely in either summer or winter, but not in both.

Spring or early summer slips are easy to root. Just take three to four-inch cuttings and insert them in a shaded box of sandy soil. Roots will form in ten to fourteen days. Then the little plants are ready to be potted separately in garden soil. The first pots are small, but by autumn the young plants will be ready for five-inch containers measured by the top diameter). If these are filled with a rather stiff, clay-soil mixture, so much the better. At all times geraniums will flower more freely if the roots are kept a little pot-bound and somewhat on the "dry" side. From these and all other flowering plants every faded blossom must be promptly nipped to make room for further development.

The wax begonias need almost no rest, but a constant gentle pruning which encourages the steady formation of new flowering growth. Weak, spindly plants are so because they are not regularly pinched back or are overwatered—the casualties from this condition always exceeding those from drought.

The nasturtiums, even this late, are products of the summer garden. Long pieces of the vines will grow for months in a vase of water if they are cut well before frost and then fed every week with a few drops of liquid manure. These blossoms follow out the color scheme for the season—pink, blue and gold.

The orange tree represents some years of growth. Florists offer such specimens, or the home gardener can grow her own, if only she will be patient. Seeds from the breakfast oranges are put to soak in warm water until they swell. Then each is planted four times in thickness deep in a three-inch pot of light, sandy soil. Growth will be slow to appear, but meanwhile the soil is kept evenly moist—not wet— and the pots set in a warm place.

Good, firm garden soil is supplied as the orange trees are gradually moved on from their first small quarters to five or six inch pots. They will flourish almost all year in a sunny window, but each February they must be rested in a cool place—forty to fifty degrees—and for a month or so watered only occasionally.

With a little forethought, the window garden at Christmas is like a pageant revealing the true spirit of the season. On Christmas Eve the sweet faces of the virgin and her kneeling angels glow in the soft light of the candles. The ruby glass is luminous, while the scent of the flowers adds to the red-and-white loveliness of the scene.

The permanent green of the picture remains, but it has been re-arranged a little to change the composition. The polypodium fern makes its first entry, while the flower of Christmas, the poinsettia, is the star in this part of the performance. And the same poinsettia may be a regular visitor if, when blossoms and leaves fall, it is removed from the window, kept dry and cool, and rested until April. Then it may be watered, to start it into growth, shaken free of two-thirds of the old soil, repotted in rich earth and kept in the outdoor garden in the sunlight until autumn. If a low plant is again desired the new growth is cut back the first week in August to within two inches of the old wood and two or three of the three or five shoots which appear are cut out. This pruning keeps the poinsettia in window bounds for another holiday season.

The kalanchoes on the table likewise bloom in ruddy tones. They are succulents of easiest culture, demanding but moderate watering and producing a long succession of coral flowers, even into summer.

Lilies of the valley will bloom at any time through the winter if cold-storage forcing pips are first thawed out and then planted in fiber, moss, sand or soil, the roots covered and the points of growth showing. The florist invariably brings them into perfection in twenty-one days; but without his facilities for careful regulation, allow about a month, planting those for Christmas near the twenty-fifth of November and placing them for the first ten to fourteen days in a dark, well-ventilated place—you can cover the tops with an inverted paper box full of holes—at about seventy degrees. When the spokes are three to four inches high the plants are ready for the light, but after the flowers appear they are shaded a little to prolong their freshness. Cared for in an out-of-the-way place until spring, they may then be made permanent residents of the outdoor garden.

For Christmas bloom, plant narcissus bulbs about November eighteenth in bowls on low layers of pebbles. The water supply is kept regularly just around the lower third of the bulbs. As growth develops, after two to three dark, cold but frost-free weeks, more pebbles are added to support the rooted plants and the bowls are moved to the light, where the yellow spears turn green in a fcw days. Then sunshine is allowed and the flower stalks shoot up. The blooms of this early series appear in five to six weeks from planting time, and success is assured if only the bulbs are not submerged in water and the plants are kept out of drafts and away from radiators. Temperatures nearer sixty than seventy degrees produce more perfect blooms. Excessively high heat results in blasting of buds. The bulbs are worthless after forcing.

At the top of this Christmas window appear the delicate, fragile blossoms of white French Roman hyacinths. These are a tender type, smaller than the familiar Dutch hyacinth and with a tendency to repeated bloom, two or three successive flowers appearing on the same bulb. For Christmas perfection, make plantings the last week in October in pebbles with just the tips of the bulbs revealed and place them, after a thorough watering, in an unheated closet where a covering of brown paper shuts out the light. Thereafter the water level is maintained, as for narcissus, around the lower third of the bulb. In about eighteen days the paper is removed, because top growth is started, but the plants are not brought to a warmer room until the fat flower cones are well developed—about seven to eight weeks from planting time. A week at the window, and the green wands are covered with white bells ringing out gay little Christmas tunes for a fortnight longer.

As the Christmas flowers fade, the begonias and geraniums which have been adorning another less conspicuous sunny window—an extra window for storing and forcing is as helpful an adjunct to the perfect indoor garden as a well-stocked pantry is to a kitchen—are brought back, until the third scene is set for St. Valentine's Day. This one is pink and lavender with three gay, mauve fairy primroses from the florist to enliven the picture.

Of a little deeper tone is the second set of French Roman hyacinths on the top shelf. This porcelain-blue variety, Virginia, is not so prompt to blossom as its paler sister, but if planted at the same time and not brought to the light until the first of February, it will slowly reveal its loveliness for St. Valentine's Day.

Two more perennials complete the gaiety of this mid-February picture—another begonia and the flamingo flowers seen at the ends of the plant table. The begonia is the variety Corallina lucerna, a large, sturdy type which from January on shakes out great umbels of rosy blossoms.

The flamingo flower, or anthurium, comes in a variety of white to red shades. Growers often class this a late-winter or early-spring flowering plant, but I have frequently had it in bloom the entire length of the window-garden season, its long rest occuring conveniently during the summer months. The buds take weeks to develop and a single exotic flower holds its perfection for months at a time.

Spring comes to the window garden with a golden gladness. The green frame now is thick and full, revealing its sense of new life in the world with numerous young shoots. Another set of lilies of the valley bears a spring message, while family Easter presents of early double tulips and glistening white cyclamens are just what the gardener hoped for to complete her spring display.

The forsythia branches, cut from the shrubbery border a week before, were forced into bloom in vases of water set here in the sunny window. The buff freesias at the top and golden callas on the floor, however, are the result of the gardener's long forethought for her Easter scene, the bulbs being purchased in the fall and stored until January in a cool place.

Toward the middle of January, after ten days of ripening on a cool but sunny window sill, freesias for Easter blooming—considering the date the second week in April—are planted in a loose, well-moistened soil mixture of garden loam, leaf mold or peat moss, and sand. The bulbs are covered with half an inch of soil and set two inches apart. A cool atmosphere of fifty-five to sixty degrees is essential during the entire growing period of approximately twelve weeks. For freesia development the unheated guest room or storeroom is ideal. At first the plantings are shaded, but when the sprouts appear the pans are moved to a sunny window, where they are still kept cool. Then frequent tepid waterings—several a day rather than a single heavy application—are advisable.

The calla, however, planted in a six-inch pot about the middle of January, can profitably spend all its days on a shelf in the sunny window garden. A rich soil, one-third of it cow manure, and an abundance of warm water after growth is well started, will bring it to perfection just about Easter Day and, once the golden chalice is formed, it will hold its proud beauty for nearly three weeks.

As the bulbs and cyclamens fade, the flowering geraniums, begonias, anthurium, kalanchoes and even the orange tree, which may be wearing spring blossoms at this season, are all assembled for an end-of-the-season curtain call. Until the middle of May, when the outdoor garden is again warm and alluring, they will perform their joyous play, delighting their sponsor with the evidences of her art.